SAINT PAUL

APOSTLE OF NATIONS

Daniel - Rops

Scepter

NIHIL OBSTAT
Rev. Robert Pelten, C.S.C., S.T.D

IMPRIMATUR
✠ John F. Noll, D.D.
Bishop of Fort Wayne, Indiana

NIHIL OBSTAT
F. Amiot p. s. s.

IMPRIMATUR
P. Brot, vic. gen.

Copyright:1952
Librairie Artheme Fayard
Paris, France

Copyright: 1953
Fides Publishers Association
21 W. Superior, Chicago 10, Illinois

Reprinted by Scepter Publishers
with permission of Claretian Publications
© 2008 Claretian Publications (Fides/Claretian).
All rights reserved.

Scepter Publishers, Inc.
P.O. Box 211, New York, N.Y. 10018
www.scepterpublishers.org
All rights reserved.

Translated by Jex Martin

ISBN-13: 978-1-59417-080-5

Contents

CHAPTER 1 / THE ENEMY OF CHRIST   1

The Deacon's Blood   1

Jewish Child in a Greek City   8

The Rabban's Pupil   16

The Way and the Light   22

CHAPTER 2 / BY ORDER OF THE HOLY SPIRIT   30

Apprenticeship   30

Christ Came for All Men   40

The Messenger of the Holy Spirit   50

CHAPTER 3 / THE GREAT ADVENTURES   60

The Gates of Faith Are Opened for Pagans   70

Discovery of Europe   82

CHAPTER 4 / THE ROAD OF SACRIFICE   96

The Wide Open Door   96

Clarion of the Spirit   106

The Road Which Leads to Calvary   116

CHAPTER 5 / THROUGH BLOOD TO ROME   125

Prisoner of Christ   136

"Bear Witness in Rome"   146

Chapter 1

ENEMY OF CHRIST

The Deacon's Blood

Through the crowded squares and stair like streets of Jerusalem a howling mob was driving a man toward death. He was a young man, full of grace and power, whose face shone with wisdom and daring and who appeared marvelously calm. He knew, nonetheless, to what he was being led; toward that terrible enclosure at the gates of the city, heaped with stones and bloodstained rocks, where for centuries rebels against the Law and adulterous women were dragged in terror. He was going to be stoned to death. But, struck, insulted, his tunic in rags, his face striped with welts, the man went on indifferent to the furious cries; his eyes on the sky, his lips murmuring prayers, he appeared to belong to the earth no longer, to have plunged already into the midst of eternity.

Some months had already passed since, on a bald hillock near another gate in the wall, in another of those nameless fields abandoned to stray dogs and vultures, a self-styled prophet had died at the order of the chiefs of the people and the princes of the priests, crucified between two thieves. All Israel had believed then that it was forever finished with Him, with His name, with His sect; that there would no longer be any discussion of Him, more than of any of those visionaries or self-proclaimed prophets who arose from time to time and in a few weeks were swallowed up. On the evening of the seventh of April in the year 30—ah! the followers of the pretended Messiah had not been heroic then! Put to flight, scattered, holed up in the slums and tombs—what resistance had they dared offer the judicial decision of the Sanhedrin? None whatsoever. And the case of the party named Jesus was disposed of permanently.

However, events had belied these conjectures. Quite soon, on the morrow of the drama on Calvary, the Galilean partisans had reappeared. Less than two months after that sinister evening when every passerby had seen the adventurer die on the gallows, the chief of His band, Simon, surnamed Peter, could be heard shouting to the people openly in the public square: "Men of Israel, hear these words. Jesus of Nazareth, him whom you have had slain by the hands of the wicked, nailing him to the cross, this man for whom God has given testimony through many acts of power, miracles, and signs wrought among you—yes, God made him Lord and Messiah, this Jesus whom you have crucified!" (Acts 2:22, 36, *passim*). What daring! To proclaim as Savior, Messiah, Glorious King of Israel, a man ignominiously condemned . . . where did these people get such faith and such presumption?

They had an answer to this question. Jesus, they declared, had not remained in death's power. The third day after His burial His tomb had been found empty. He had appeared to His faithful, first to one or another alone, then to groups more and more numerous. For forty days He had lived anew upon the earth, a mysterious, supernatural life; in a way He was perfectly similar to mortal men, since He could be touched and had been seen to eat bread and fish, but at the same time He was endowed with strange, disconcerting powers, passing through closed doors and appearing suddenly in the four corners of Palestine. This second life of Jesus had ended in a still more surprising fashion: one fine spring day, on the Hill of the Olive Trees, while He was still instructing His friends, He had risen toward Heaven as if an irresistible force within Him was carrying Him off, and He had disappeared before their astonished eyes.

It was on this that the faith of the Galileans rested. It was what Peter had said when he spoke to the assembled people: "Him whom you crucified, God has raised him up; he has broken for him the bonds of death. We are all witnesses to it!" (Acts 2:23). And this unbelievable affirmation, this proclamation of such an absurd fact, was being made by an increasing number of men and women. They went from house to house, from group to group, communicating their faith in the Resurrected One, recalling His exemplary life, and teaching the fundamentals of His doctrine. Since Pentecost, especially, they had been full of audacity. That morning, when all Israel was commemorating the revelation made to Moses, while the Galileans were gathered together, another bizarre phenomenon had taken place: outside it manifested itself in a terrible wind, bursting out of a completely calm sky; within the house, where they all were together, they had seen, they declared, tongues like fire appear and descend to rest on each one of them; the work of the Holy Spirit! It was then, for the first time, that they dared to cry out that they belonged to Christ, that they would henceforth be witnesses of His Word. It was since then that they had lost all fear, all reserve. And—a miracle—when they were teaching of these things, everyone understood them in his own language, and the hearts of many were stirred on hearing them.

Thus the little sect of Galileans had begun to win supporters. When Peter had spoken on the threshold of the Cenacle on Pentecost, a certain number of those present had been strongly moved; they had repented having approved the juridical murder of the Son of Man and had asked to receive that visible mark of pardon which was called baptism. A little later, the miraculous cure by two of Christ's faithful, Peter and John, of a cripple squatting in the gateway to the Temple had completed the effect of their preaching; the number of baptized had increased. Indeed, the number was not yet very impressive—a few hundred, perhaps at the maximum a few thousand. A small matter, in truth, this handful of non-conformists in the entirely Jewish community: a community ranged round its government of priests, vigilant guardians of strict observances and of the Law; and still less in the gigantic Roman Empire of which the Promised Land was a canton, that Empire stretching from Scotland to Egypt, from the Caucasus to the Sahara, and over which reigned—harsh, suspicious, prompt with sanctions and cruel punishment—the sad old man of the Isle of Capri, Tiberius. But this diminutive sect knew that it was promised the highest destiny; the grain of mustard seed, as the Master had said, knew that it would become a tree; and hearts were exalted by this conviction.

In truth, Rome was in no way interested in the little sect that vaunted a crucified visionary. The Procurator Pontius Pilate, who represented the Emperor, always on the alert in his fortress-palace, the Antonia, had limited himself to maintaining order, brutally if needed, among the Jewish people, whom he took to be absurd, incomprehensible, and unbearable. Jesus had died because the public order had been disturbed through His fault. All was calm again, and Pilate hoped it would remain so. But this was not the case in the Israelite community itself, where everything that involved religion produced a great stir. The Scribes and Doctors of the Law, who had been among the effective agents of the plot which had destroyed Jesus, were not without some mistrust as they saw the little group of His disciples gaining proselytes. The two clans who disputed the leadership of Israel, the Sadducees and the Pharisees, while each hated the other, found themselves in agreement on one point: that such propaganda was not to be allowed to take on importance.

So, when Peter and John began to speak, after the miraculous cure of the cripple at the Temple, they were arrested. It was a vain attempt to silence them. With an unfailing tranquility they cried: "We cannot be silent about these things!" And when they had been reproached for breaking the laws of the community, they had replied with these words of blasphemous pride: "We must obey God rather than men." Rabbi Gamaliel, one of the most respected among the Doctors of the Law, intervened and prevented the violent from taking too severe measures against Peter and John. But could the people of the Sanhedrin forget that these men had said explicitly that the blood of the just man Jesus would fall upon them? Could they permit the Galilean propaganda to work upon their followers and to gain adherents, even among the priests? (Acts 6:7). This theocracy, this dictatorship of the high clergy and theologians which was the Israelite community of the time, could not tolerate innovators or nonconformists if its own foundations were to remain firm. The conflict between the leaders of the Jewish people and those holding the new doctrine was fatal. It broke out between the years 32 and 36.

This is what happened. In the community of Jesus' followers, the Church of Christ, new problems were created by the constantly increasing number of adherents. The leaders designated by the Master, the Apostles, found themselves more and more occupied with evangelistic tasks, which were beginning to reach beyond the limits of the Holy City and to extend into various places in Palestine. There was thus less time for the more modest works of administration, social action, and relations with the faithful. Still these matters did require attention, for, even in this young Church, full of fervor and love, where communal ties were secured by the most fraternal charity, certain concrete problems were arising. As always happens in human groupings, certain frictions were becoming manifest, notably with regard to the distribution of alms. These difficulties were appearing especially among the Judaizers, Jesus' followers of Palestinian origin, and the Hellenists, those who had originated in the Jewish colonies scattered through the Near East. To assume these administrative functions and to control these relations and distributions, the Apostles decided to call upon auxiliaries, the *deacons*. Seven of these were appointed.

They were all young and energetic men, chosen for these functions by very reason of their spirit of boldness and decision. One of them was named Stephen—*Stephanos* in Greek, and the name alone suffices to show that he had come from one of the great Hellenic cities where Christianity was beginning to take root. His zeal and eloquence soon attracted attention. Not content with carrying out the administrative and social duties entrusted to him, he wished to take part in the great work of propaganda. He was seen haranguing groups not only under the portal of Solomon, in the Temple court, and on street corners, but even penetrating the synagogues of the Hellenistic Jews of Cyrene, Antioch, Asia, and Cilicia, and engaging in controversy with them. With the ardor of youth, he spared nothing and no one. While Peter, in his addresses, sought to persuade his listeners, explaining to them that Jesus was indeed the expected Messiah, Stephen stressed the most abrupt, violent, and, in short, the most revolutionary elements of the Master's teaching: "No one pours new wine into old wine skins. No one sews a patch of raw cloth on an old garment" (Matt. 9:16–17). The old skins and outworn tunics sensed clearly that they were the targets of the attack, and the deacon Stephen was denounced to the Sanhedrin.

The moment was favorable for the Jewish religious leaders to attempt a check on the Galileans' propaganda. The Procurator Pontius Pilate was no longer at the Antonia; following a rather obscure affair which took place in Samaria and in which his violent methods had led to a small massacre, he had been denounced to the Syrian legate Vitellius, the future emperor, who, quite familiar with the methods of his subordinate, had sent him off to make his explanations at Rome. His successor had not yet arrived in Jerusalem. The hour was favorable then for the arrest, judgment, and execution of a man without the Romans being able to enforce their law aimed at controlling all death sentences pronounced by Jewish tribunals. The deacon Stephen was therefore arrested and the supreme tribunal convened.

The procedure was flagrantly illegal: convicted of blasphemy, Stephen could only be condemned to death; but without Roman authority, the penalty could not be executed. The trial, then, was merely a secret plan for arousing the people against the followers of Jesus, perhaps for provoking an uprising in which the accused would be massacred. The plan succeeded marvelously well. It is true that Stephen did nothing to prevent it. Faced with these men whom he would not acknowledge as judges, he remained sublimely steadfast. The prospect of shedding his blood for Christ exalted his spirit, and his face shone with something like an anticipated reduction of Paradise. Did they accuse him of blasphemy? Come now, he was the real accuser! "Stiff-necked and uncircumcised in heart and ear, you always oppose the Holy Spirit; as your fathers did, so you do also. Which of the prophets have not your fathers persecuted? And they killed those who foretold the coming of the Just One, of whom you have now been the betrayers and murderers, you who received the Law as an ordinance of angels and did not keep it!" (Acts 7:51–53).

This was too much for them! There was grinding of teeth, spectacular rending of garments; the Sanhedrites were outraged, and their fury brought floods of insults to their lips. But Stephen the deacon, with eyes lifted and with beaming countenance, belonged no more to this world. While the crazy horde summoned by the priests took hold of him and led him to the torture, he murmured in a voice of ecstasy: "I see the heavens opened, and the Son of Man standing at the right hand of God" (Acts 7:56).

Reaching the terrible place of the stoning, Stephen fell upon his knees. Around him the mob continued the death howl. According to the Law, the witnesses who had accused him, those responsible for his conviction, were supposed to cast the first stones. At arm's length they raised the blocks, the heaviest they could manage, and flung them at the martyr. On head, chest, back, and face, the stones, large and small, struck incessantly. The deacon did not cry out, did not protest. For an instant he prayed: "Lord Jesus, receive my spirit." Then he fell to the ground, his face crushed by a block. He was heard to cry once more in a loud voice: "Lord, do not lay this sin against them." Then he was still, asleep in the eternal love.

A little way off from the place where this crime was occurring, a young man stood motionless, as if rigid with emotion. Not handsome: small, ruddy, with shaggy beard and bandy legs. Every few minutes he nervously wiped the back of his hand across his brow and the top of his head, where the hair was getting thin. Features tense, teeth clenched on his lips, gaze fixed, he watched the scene with avid interest. At his feet lay a heap of garments, those of the executioners who, in order to be more at ease, had taken them off and which the spectator had offered to take care of. From his austere tunic, his long tassels, and the phylacteries that he wore on his wrists, those little leathern boxes containing verses from the Bible, his profession could be readily recognized. He was a student of religious science, a pupil of the rabbis, a guardian of the holy Law. He was a native of Tarsus in Cilicia, and his name was Saul.

A Jewish Child in a Greek City

Close to the tip of the maritime angle formed by Northern Syria and Asia Minor, the city of Tarsus was, at the beginning of our era, a small-scale replica of Alexandria or Piraeus. The prodigious commercial activity which for three centuries, since the Hellenization of the Orient by Alexander, had animated all the East Mediterranean coasts, had turned a modest Hittite and Phoenician town into a commercial center of the first rank. The location was remarkably propitious in the first place. Guardian of the route dug out of the living rock which, through the passes of the Taurus—the famous Cilician Gates— led to the plateaus of Outer Asia, Byzantium, and the West, Tarsus was linked to the sea—or rather to its port of Regmon— by a magnificent river of pure cool water, the Cydnus, sung by all the poets.

The modern visitor, attracted by the historic associations of the place, finds it difficult to realize its splendid past. From the shabby port of Mersina to the city, where gardens and orchards once displayed the multiple splendor of their harvests, all that remains are sinister swamps and wretched prairies. Tarsus itself is no more than a sleepy Turkish township of some twenty thousand souls, cut off from the sea by alluvial deposits and disdained by the main line of the railroads. Where is its glory of yesteryear? Where is the bright Cydnus, diverted from the city by the emperor Justinian? Where are the luxurious residences that once gleamed on the hill? Where are the temples, the baths, the theaters? Is this the city which naively boasted that it went back to the Homeric heroes, to Semiramis or Sardanapalus, if not to Perseus, or, indeed, Aphrodite? In this feverish bottom land, amid the rushes and daffodils at the foot of the rugged mountain, one needs much imagination to picture Alexander the Great camping on the river bank in order to bathe; Cicero, the governor of the land, passing in a long cortege with his twenty-four lictors; and the disquieting Egyptian marvel, the adolescent Cleopatra, disembarking in secret and lightly clad from her golden trireme with the purple sails, with the aim of seducing Antony, the Roman conqueror.

In the mass of the population of Tarsus, which two thousand years ago may have numbered some three hundred thousand souls, the ethnic elements were extremely diverse. On the old Assyro-Iranian base had been superimposed mountaineers from Asia Minor, Bedouins from Syria, Greeks from everywhere; in short, that indefinable melange which one still finds today in all the Mediterranean ports, with the worst and the best side by side. "An admirable people, intelligent and industrious": thus a Strabo, a Dion Chrysostom, an Ammianus Marcellinus had spoken of the Tarsiotes. Dio Cassius, on the other hand, had regarded them as "the worst of races"; and both opinions were very likely accurate.

Among these heterogeneous elements one group was remarkable for its cohesion and aloofness—the Jews. For centuries the sons of Israel, who were notably prolific, had sent out nuclei of emigrants practically everywhere in the known world. In this Diaspora some descended from deportees dispersed by the fatalities of history; others were businessmen, bankers, export-import specialists, or even soldiers, expatriated to earn a living. Didn't the Sibylline Oracles say of Israel: "The entire earth is full of thee and even the sea"? Rome numbered fifty thousand Jews, Alexandria two hundred thousand. The Tarsiote colony, developed mainly since the year 175 before our era, when the Seleucid king, Antiochus Epiphanes, had taken Jewish mercenaries into his army, was certainly quite numerous. As elsewhere, it was probably strongly united, very closely organized, with its own leaders, its customs, its tribunals, and its "house of doctrine" or synagogue, where all the members of the community came together. It was undoubtedly not isolated materially, set apart in a ghetto as it was to be in the medieval West; but morally it led a somewhat withdrawn life, little inclined to fuse with the idolatrous masses. It was in the frame of this Jewish nucleus set up on Hellenic soil that Saul was born.

In the courtyard of an old house in Tarsus they still show, under a little shed, a very ancient well which is called "the Well of Saint Paul." Its marble curb, a low one, is deeply grooved by the rubbing of the rope; its water is cool and sweet. Its name, we are assured, derives from the fact that there was once drawn from its depths a black stone on which an unskillful hand had inscribed *Paulos*. It would be too ingenious to suppose that this humble pebble was inscribed by Saul as a child . . .

In any case, it was in some such house—they can hardly have changed much—that the future Apostle of the Gentiles first saw the light of day. On what date we cannot say with any certainty. The two lone indications furnished by the texts are vague; besides, they don't quite agree with each other. In the Acts of the Apostles, when he relates the stoning of Stephen, Saint Luke speaks of Paul as a "young man," an elastic term which might fit a boy of twenty as well as a man of twenty-seven or twenty-eight. In the Epistle to Philemon, on the other hand, Saint Paul calls himself old. A "young man" in the year 36, an "old man" in 62—this scarcely seems reconcilable if, at the time of Stephen's death, Saul was still almost an adolescent. Many have admitted, therefore, that he may have been born some fifteen years after Christ, between the years 8 and 10 of our era, but this assertion rests on conjecture.

On his family, at least, we are better informed. It certainly had a status of some prominence in Tarsus, for Saul was born a citizen of the city and his father was one already. In the Jewish community it was respected, for its connections had been duly certified and its children could call themselves indisputably "Hebrews, sons of Hebrews, of the race of Israel, offspring of Abraham, of the tribe of Benjamin" (Acts 22:3; 2 Cor. 11:22; Phil. 3:5). How long had the forebears of the Apostle been established there? One tradition—very debatable though related by Saint Jerome—would make them natives of Giscala in Galilee, brought into Cilicia as slaves or prisoners of war at the time when the legions of Varus (4 B.C.) had reestablished order in northern Palestine by dint of sweeping devastation and deportation. At any rate, if this origin can be accepted as true, we must admit that these exiles had certainly managed to rehabilitate themselves.

The industry in which Saul's father had prospered was one of those which had made the fortune of the great Cilician port, that of textiles; "cilices" they called them in those days and the word is still in use as a term for certain coarse, puckered fabrics. The materials woven from the hair of the Taurus goats were undoubtedly rather coarse, but they were waterproof and practically impossible to wear out; from these rude fabrics they made up carpets, tents, and those cloaks worn by shepherds and caravan leaders, known in our days as *kepeniks*. Saul's father was thus *skenopoios*, *tabernacularius*, a merchant craftsman of tents. A modest trade in appearance, more artisanry than industry, and which in our time would not assure its practitioner much social status; but we must remember that Israel lacked completely that scorn for manual labor which the Greeks and Romans affected, and that it was even customary for intellectuals—the Doctors of the Law, for example—to be artisans or workmen, carpenters like Rabbi Hillel, blacksmiths like Rabbi Isaac, stewards like Rabbi Oschia. And besides, a tentmaker in Tarsus probably made money.

It is in the paternal workshop, then, located in some lane in the business section of the city, that we must picture Saul as a child. The long glossy threads, gleaming black, stretch out and interweave with dreamlike rapidity. The heavy card of polished wood, operated by a chain, moves back and forth with regular strokes. The shuttle flies across the red woof. Destined to succeed his father, according to the tradition of his race, Saul learns the trade of tent making, that trade which he is later to practice as a simple workman and no more as a master; when he chooses to risk all to follow Christ, and in the course of his greatest adventures, he will depend on this to earn his living. This work in his father's shop probably continued until he was about fourteen years old.

A little Jewish boy, raised in a profoundly Jewish environment—such is the future Apostle. Still, there is more to it than that. The son of the Torah lives in a Greek city and this fact will be of capital importance. From earliest childhood his double name has characterized what his destiny will be. When, on the eighth day after his birth, his parents had him circumcised according to the Law, he received an old Israelite name, a name highly honored in the tribe of Benjamin, the same, in fact, that the first king of Israel had borne: *Schaoul, Saul,* which has the sense of "the desired." However—we know of this through numerous papyri and inscriptions—the Jews settled in Hellenic lands generally took a Greek name, which they used in their relations with pagan society. *Saulos* would hardly have been suitable, for in the Hellenic tongue the word suggests a man who sways on his feet or waddles. *Paulos* was better; it recalled the glorious *yens paulinia* of the Roman annals, and it is not too unlikely that some ancestor of the Apostle received the right to use it from an authentic Paulus. "Saul, also called Paul," Saint Luke was to say in speaking of his master (Acts 13:9); the child of Tarsus was to bear the two names until the end.

This was a concrete symbol of his double spiritual inheritance. On one hand, the child Saul grew up in a Jewish environment, profoundly faithful; but on the other hand, little Paulos was thrown into contact with all the Greco-Roman elements in his native city. Did the two influences harmonize? Certainly the first was deeper and more effective. His family belonged to the sect of the Pharisees, who piqued themselves on "raising the hedge of the Law still higher." At home, nothing but Aramaic was spoken, the common language of the Jews of the time, that which Jesus had used; and they knew enough Hebrew to recite their prayers in the sacred tongue. While quite young the child was brought into the presence of the Eternal and of His message, contained in the Book of Books; such was the pedagogy prescribed by the *Opinions of the Fathers:* "at five years to read the Bible; at ten years to study the Mishna, the tradition of the Ancients; at thirteen to observe all the precepts."

As a small boy, then, Saul was trained to read the holy text, to meditate on the Commandments of God, to know the history of his people—a glorious and sorrowful history— and especially to live in strict observance of the Law. All through his life, even when he had become a Christian, he was to be marked by his first training. "Salvation is from the Jews," Jesus had cried (John 4:22), and no one was more convinced than Saul of the truth of these words; he would never disown his race, and even when he had suffered so much at the hands of his former co-religionists he was to utter that cry of wonderful loyalty: "I could wish to be anathema myself from Christ for the sake of my brethren, who are my kinsman according to the flesh" (Rom. 9:3). Such is the first principle of his training—the most essential, the most profound. But there were others.

In the great city the Jewish child could not escape daily
encounter with the Hellenic world, its spectacles, its forms of
culture. The son of a merchant, he must have—while still a
child—learned Greek in order to speak with the customers—
a fluent, familiar Greek, which he acquired alone, without
teachers. Though he was kept apart from the little pagans by
austere paternal discipline, it was scarcely possible for him to
avoid meeting boys of his age from other environments, nor
was it possible for a youngster as intelligent and quick-witted
as he was to remain indifferent to the manifestations of an
extremely civilized society. While he rejected its influence,
the Hellenic world must have acted upon him secretly, as
through osmosis.

This may be discerned in reading his texts. His letters will
be full of allusions to Tarsiote life, references to city affairs,
commerce, law, the army: all this is extremely different from
the style of Jesus, who, as a man of the Galilean people, constantly referred to the fields, nature, the splendor of plants,
the free flight of birds. Quite naturally, Paul will borrow his
comparisons from the stadium games, races, wrestling bouts
in the arena, and discussions in the agora. From time to time
he will quote from Aratos the Stoic, Menander, and
Epimenides; he will not have read the texts perhaps, but such
quotations had probably become proverbial among the
Greek people in Tarsus.

Must we admit a still more profound influence? In the religious order, certainly not. For the pious little Jew, brought up
on rigid principles, Hellenistic paganism must have inspired
horror. When the mad processions of flutists and lute players
passed through the streets; when the crowd howled as the
crackling fire burned the pine tree effigy of Old Baal Sandam
(identified by the Greeks with Heracles), and they waited for a
young tree, symbol of reborn vegetation, to take his place;
when the zealots of the Persian god Mithra had themselves
baptized with the blood of a bull, a follower of Yahweh could
feel nothing but disgust. When, later, he makes an allusion to

the terrible absence which lies in the soul of those who live "without God in the world" (Eph. 2:12), he knows exactly what he wants to say. Paganism had enlightened him on its shortcomings and mediocrities.

But there was more in Tarsus besides these cults of aberrant mysticism into which the old religion was breaking up. The city was a great university center, "surpassing Athens and Alexandria in its love of the sciences," Strabo was to say; and he added that one saw Tarsiote intellectuals throughout the Empire. Some of the Masters who taught in the great Cilician port had played prominent roles: Athenodorus, who had been one of the teachers of Augustus and whom the latter had sent to Tarsus to reorganize public life and administration; Nestor, another philosopher, who had also been called to court to educate the little son of the Emperor, Marcellus. The mighty shades of Zeno of Cyprus, Aratos of Cilicia, Chrysippus, and Apollonius, all illustrious Stoics, were still hovering over Tarsus when Saul grew up there. Even if—as is probable—he never frequented the Greek schools, nor really studied the philosophy which Seneca was to bring into fashion, he must have measured its importance, at least, and, in taking a stand against it, defined more clearly his own position. Though exerted *a contrario*, this Greek influence was not to be lost: it was to make Paul conscious of the importance of culture; it was to show him that faith is faced with certain problems which must be solved by the intellect; it was to orientate him in the very path in which his genius was to flower.

The world which surrounded his youth taught him one other great reality: the Empire. His father was a Roman citizen, and he himself was one by birth. In those days, for provincials like the Tarsiotes, this was a rare and envied privilege; it was to remain so for almost two centuries more, until 212 when, for fiscal reasons, the emperor Caracalla was to bestow it on all the freemen of the Empire. A Roman citizen was a privileged person; he possessed full civil rights; he was authorized—even if he could not materially do so—to go to Rome to elect the magistrates. He was protected to a certain extent against despotic officials, who could not inflict on him either corporal punishment, such as flagellation, or dishonoring torture, such as crucifixion: had not Cicero, a century before, had Verres condemned because he had crucified a Roman citizen in Sicily? How did the family of Saul obtain this famous title? Had they bought it—very dearly—as was done in rare cases? Or perhaps, in the political struggles at the beginning of the century, his ancestors had been in a position to flatter or to offer real aid to a Julius Caesar, or a Mark Antony. In any case, the Apostle was to take pride in bearing it; on many occasions he was to claim its rights and prerogatives. And this direct dependence on the Empire was to have a profound significance for him, well expressed in chapter thirteen of the Epistle to the Romans: in the Roman domination he was to see not only an instrument of oppression—as so many of the Church's faithful did—but a positive grandeur, a powerful and beneficent organization, whose existence derived from the designs of Providence. Through this, as through his relations with the Greek world, the future converter of the nations was being made ready.

The Rabban's Pupil

At fourteen or fifteen, then, Saul was a young Jewish boy, trained in the disciplines of his race but whose eyes were opening on broader horizons. It was then that his father sent him to Jerusalem. This was probably in the year 22 or 23 of our era. Was it not further said in the *Opinions of the Fathers:* "at fifteen years let the child apply himself to learning the Talmud"? For a young Jew, to follow religious studies was not only to become perfect in theology and Biblical science, but to attain to the rank of savant, scribe, and man of letters, and to receive all the consideration attached to these titles of prestige. On his return to his country the student of the rabbis would have, quite naturally, a prominent place in the Jewish community; he would be called "Doctor" or "Master." The sojourn in the Holy City was thus an essential step, and Saul's father had the intelligence to bring his son to make it. Long as the route was from Cilicia to Judea, and however difficult his separation from his loved ones and his lonely life in the holy capital, Saul must have accepted this test with fervor.

Jerusalem had always been—since the time of King David, a thousand years before—the spiritual fatherland of every believing Jew. To its Temple crowds of pilgrims went up for the Passover and the great feasts, singing Psalms of love and desire. These were the ramparts lamented by the exiles of Babylon when they sat by the rivers and sent up the sublime cry: "If I forget you, Jerusalem, may my right hand be forgotten! May my tongue cleave to my palate if I remember you not!" To her there came, from all the Jewish communities of the Diaspora, thousands of students eager to hear the word of the Masters in this place where the Spirit surely dwelt.

Saul was one of these pupils of the rabbis. The student life of Jerusalem was often noisy and always enthusiastic, but it also had much of that gravity and earnestness which one sees in the men of the race. One worked diligently in the Holy City. The instruction was given here, there, and everywhere: in private houses, in the synagogues, more often in the open air, under the portico of the Temple, a few steps from the Holy of Holies. There, under the colonnade, the students formed a circle around a master, squatting together in a huddle as one still sees the Muslim students of the great university El-Azar in Cairo; and they listened tirelessly. A popular professor drew the students to him in droves; such were, at the beginning of the century, Rabbi Judas and Rabbi Matthias, whose rivalry had been famous. Some of the great names of the Doctors of the Law were known to the ends of the Diaspora; for example, Hillel and Shammai, who were to have a profound influence on Jewish tradition; Shammai the rigorous, Hillel broader and more liberal, and their two trends clashed in resounding encounters. Interpretation of a text aroused as much excitement as a boxing match or murder case in our day.

The Bible was the only end and the sole means of instruction. One studied its sentences, less to explain them literally than to extract arguments useful in debates. Learned calculations were made on the number of words and their equivalents, calculations which were to be the basis of the Kabala. One drew from the text not only religious knowledge, but also, through an exegetical interpretation called "searching" (*midrash*), one could extract moral principles and historical lessons, known as "the way" (*halacha*) and "the doctrine" (*hagada*). These "hagadic" methods appear strange and fantastic to us today, but the least of the rabbis took them extremely seriously. The study of the *Mishna* and the *Talmud*, in which the commentaries of the Fathers were collected, was supposed to complete that of the inspired Book and to form an inexhaustible arsenal of contradictory arguments. In a discussion, the more Biblical quotations one could muster to support his thesis, the more he was appreciated.

Instruction was given in the form of rhythmic, cadenced developments, which the student was suppose to learn by heart, without taking notes. It would have been a grave error not to repeat a rabbi's lesson in the same terms he had used. "A good student," assures the Talmud, "must be like a staunch cistern, which lets not a single drop of water escape." Saul spent years in this way, a student at the feet of a master, repeating and droning out his sayings and sentences, becoming impregnated with the sacred text to his very bones. Among his comrades there may well have been one or another of those whom we shall find associated with him later in his work: the excellent Barnabas, his first companion on the road, Silas or Silvanus, a distinguished member of the community in Jerusalem, who was to accompany him on his second mission. This has been a subject for conjecture, as well as whether Saul's violence against Stephen might not have had its origin in an antagonism between two young men who knew each other only too well.

The master whose courses Saul followed was Gamaliel. He belonged to the sect of the Pharisees, to which the family of the young Tarsiote gave allegiance, and which had in its hands at this time practically all the higher religious education. They descended from those *hassidim* who in recent centuries had been the soul of resistance to paganism; they were a sort of puritans, one might say, austere, savage, securely anchored to unshakable convictions and rigid observances. On the Mosaic precepts and their interpretation the Pharisees multiplied glosses and opinions. The commandment "thou shalt keep holy the Sabbath" had given rise to entire volumes of commentaries on what one might do or not do on this sacred day. For example, they gravely asked if one had the right to eat an egg the greater part of which had issued from the chicken before the second star appeared, for from all the evidence, the chicken had broken the Sabbath by laying. A rabbinical treatise declared that on the consecrated day it was as serious to squash a flea as to kill a camel. To which the broader Rabbi Zamuel replied that he saw no harm in cutting off its feet. If Saul learned much from his Pharisee masters, it is not unreasonable to think that he was also aware of the desiccating influence of this stereotyped and formalistic teaching. Perhaps he had then a presentiment of that truth he was to learn later: "the letter kills, but the spirit gives life."

Gamaliel was certainly the most remarkable member of the Pharisee sect. He was an heir, by blood as well as by convictions, of the great Hillel, and, like him, represented the broader tendencies. He was good-natured and affable, and despised no one. He did not condemn the believers who spoke Greek; he did not ostentatiously turn away his head when a pagan woman crossed his path in the street; he even deigned to return a stranger's greeting, which was regarded as a remarkable token of generosity. And still his orthodoxy was irreproachable, and was so universally recognized that a new term was coined to attest it. Whereas, previously, the Doctors of the Law were called *rah* ("master"), or else *rabbi* ("my master"), he was accorded the title of "our master" (*rabban*). At his death a eulogy was prepared which was so fervent that it was gathered into the Mishna: "Since Gamaliel disappeared the honor of the Law is no more; with him died purity and piety."

It could scarcely be denied that Rabban Gamaliel had a deeply religious soul and a sound conscience. When Peter and John were arrested, one voice rose to defend them in the midst of the Sanhedrin, that of Gamaliel; he addressed his colleagues with a speech reported in the Book of Acts: "Keep away from these men and let them alone. For if this plan or work is of men, it will be overthrown; but if it is of God, you will not be able to overthrow it" (Acts 5:38–39). And thanks to him, the Apostles were released. This is obviously no reason for admitting, as they did in the Middle Ages, that Rabban Gamaliel ended his days a Christian, but it is beyond doubt that such a man must have had a profound influence on a liberal mind like Saul's. A doctrinal influence, first of all, for the Pharisees believed in the immortality of the soul, Providence, free will, the resurrection of the dead, the judgment of the just and unjust; still more, an influence of spiritual enthusiasm and orientation in life, for with them religion was the end and the means of everything, faith was the very core of existence, and nothing that happened escaped the eye of God. Saul the Pharisee was never to forget these lessons.

When, after six or seven years of study and approaching his twenty-first year, he returned to Tarsus to assist his father in his work, he certainly did not renounce that love of God and passion for the absolute which he had developed under the influence of a revered teacher. Industry and commerce could not fill the life of a discerning mind, and besides, the *Opinions of the Fathers* had put him on guard against the danger of letting himself become absorbed by his tasks: "Who gives himself too much to commerce," said the sober Hillel, "acquires no wisdom." Following the precept of Rabbi Shammai, Saul undoubtedly "made the study of the Law the rule of existence." Respected by the whole Jewish community of his native city, he not only gave an example of what it was to live according to God, but he spoke in the synagogues, took part in the liturgical offices, gave juridical advice, and solved cases of conscience, for all these things were expected of the rabbis.

Perhaps it was the desire to plunge again into the flowing spring of his studious youth, to receive the advice of his teachers, which brought him back to Jerusalem a few years later. Between his first and his second sojourn in the Holy City, events had moved on. In March of the year 28 a young Galilean, until then completely unknown outside His village of Nazareth, had come forth, traveled about the high roads, and announced to the masses a new Word. According to Him, the Kingdom of God was near at hand, and to prepare for its coming it was necessary to cleanse one's soul, put off the old man, and be transformed. In the eyes of this Prophet, formal precepts were of less account than right intention and purity of heart. Jesus was truly the living contradiction of the Pharisees He rudely derided. Could it be that a man like Saul, of fiery temperament, easily led to extremes, would experience anything but a feeling of horror and rage when confronted with these affirmations of the Galilean? The fanaticism of the Law, which the self-styled Messiah attacked, must have boiled up in him like acid. If some sincere souls had accepted this doctrine, it was but one more reason for Saul to detest Him. And the execution of Jesus, willed and determined by the Pharisees of the Sanhedrin, he could only see as legal and necessary. Throughout his formative years he was to be the enemy of Christ.

Had he met Him? Had he seen and heard Him? It is more than doubtful. The dates of Jesus' stays in the Holy City and that of his future Apostle do not agree. When Paul later affirmed that he saw Him, it was in a special sense, with reference to the manifestation on the road to Damascus, perhaps more in the spirit than according to the flesh. And, if the young Pharisee was present in Jerusalem during the drama of April in the year 30, how are we to imagine him taking no part in it, and how are we to explain why the Gospel does not mention him? When he returned to Judea some three or four years after the death of Christ, he must have been indignant at finding adepts of the new doctrine, not only among the little people, the commoners, the despised *am-ha-arez*, but also among the intellectuals, the scribes, and perhaps his former comrades; a fiery nature like his could not remain neutral: executioner or victim, persecutor or persecuted—thus was his dilemma formulated. Such as he was then, he would choose the first alternative.

And so his attitude at the time of Stephen's martyrdom is logically explained. In approving the murder, he was undoubtedly following his conscience, if not his heart. Out of horror and scorn for the cross, he was to battle the Nazarenes, those who supported the condemned man. "I acted ignorantly," he said later (1 Tim. 1:13). There is no need to imagine what he did, what role he assumed in the persecution that followed the death of the deacon, for he has related it himself: "I persecuted this Way (of Christ) even to the death, binding and committing to prisons both men and women, as the High Priest can bear me witness, and all the elders. In fact I received letters from them to the brethren in Damascus, and I was on my way to arrest those who were there and bring them back to Jerusalem for punishment" (Acts 22:3; and cf. 9:1, 2; 26:12).

But on the road to Damascus his destiny was awaiting him.

The Way and the Light

It was a summer day, towards noon. Escorted by a troop of guards assigned to aid him in his task, Saul, tense and feverish, arrived in sight of the Syrian oasis. A full week had passed since he left the Holy City, a week of trudging along the sandy trail, including the obligatory stops for the Sabbath repose. He was in haste to reach Damascus, accomplish his mission, and assuage his anger. Neither the harsh sun nor the insidious damp nights had been able to delay him.

Two roads led to Damascus from Jerusalem. One traversed the length of Palestine, through Samaria and Galilee as far as Caesarea Philippi, then passed around Hermon and continued on straight across the steppes. The other, a shorter road, went down from Sichem toward Scythopolis, passed through the Greek city of Hippos on the shore of the Lake of Tiberias and then climbed towards the pastures of Bachan and Trachonitis, beyond which it rejoined the first route. Supposedly, the route through the Palestinian hills must have been preferable to the other, which would have required a long trek through the Jordan Valley, where in July and August temperatures of 115° are common. But even on the heights the Palestinian summer is harsh and severe, more killing than the winter.

For eight days Saul had been tramping, in dust and rubble, under a bright blue sky. Through the dried grass one could see the rugged skin of the hills and their skeleton of rocks. Everything was gray, monotonously gray; the thickets along the road, the houses in the villages, the pebbles in the wadis; and in the meager shade of the olive trees, the wool of the sheep blended with the gray of the soil.

As he traveled along, Saul continued to nurse his bile. Never, says Pascal, do we do wrong so completely and so merrily as when moved by conscience. Was he happy—this young Pharisee who was journeying to Damascus to carry out a terrible mission? But he was sure that he was acting out of conscience. The firm conviction that he was sustaining the truth merged in his heart with the restless bile of vengeance and ill humor; what personal account was he settling with this Messiah whose followers he persecuted? Would he himself have been able to analyze his feelings?

What he had done to the Nazarenes in Jerusalem was no longer enough for him. To track them down, denounce them, have them arrested and beaten with rods, force the weakest to apostatize, and, as he admitted himself, to surpass all the other young Pharisees in violence—all this still seemed insufficient (Acts 8:3; 22:4; 26:10–11; Gal. 1:13; 1 Tim. 1:13). Groups of the new doctrine's followers were forming outside of Palestine, especially in the Jewish communities of Syria; he had determined to bring them into the open and strike them down.

The High Priests to whom Paul—"breathing threats of slaughter" (Acts 9:1)—went to explain his project, evidently received him on good terms. Who was it? Was the High Priest still Caiphas, one of the saddest heroes of the scandalous trial of Christ, who, by dint of diplomatic cunning and servility had managed to maintain himself in the Pontificate some eighteen years and was not deposed until sometime in the year 36? Or was it Jonathan, one of his immediate successors, who wore the miter only six months; or Theophilus, elected in the beginning of 37? It matters little; the order for the mission was signed, directing the synagogues of Damascus to deliver to Saul their members who followed Jesus of Nazareth, to be brought back to Sion in chains.

The affair was illegal, according to both Jewish and Roman law. In principle the High Priest had no power over the local Sanhedrins of the communities of the Diaspora. But it goes without saying that his prestige was considerable and that he was quite capable of abusing it. As for the Romans, in normal times it would hardly have been tolerable for a little rabbi to go beyond the territory entrusted to the procurator of Judea and proceed to make arrests in Syria, under the very noses of their magistrates. But—and this is one of the arguments for dating the events of the year 36, when Pilate, recalled to Rome, had not yet been replaced—the occupying authority was then represented only by the administrator of Caesarea and by Vitellius, the powerful but remote legate in Syria, who, moreover, had a political understanding with the Sanhedrin authorities. If executed quickly, the coup was likely to succeed.

Thus everything contributed to Saul's haste. His brow was feverish with the overwhelming heat of the trail. He had almost reached his goal. On his left, Hermon, "firstborn of the Heights," thrust skyward its snowy peak, that peak where the transfigured Christ shone before the eyes of His followers. On his right, the Hauran hills, mauve and blue, surged towards Asia. Soon the oasis would appear, green with its palms. The air was opaque, heavy, motionless, as it is in the deserts at high noon.

Suddenly a light from heaven shone round him, surpassing the sun in intensity. The traveler fell to the ground, and he heard a voice saying, "Saul, Saul, why do you persecute me?" Stammering, he said: "Who are thou, Lord?" And the voice resumed: "I am Jesus, whom you are persecuting." Stunned and trembling, the Pharisee murmured: "Lord, what will you have me do?" And the ineffable voice continued: "Rise and go into the city, and you will be told what to do" (Acts 9:3–6).

This was a prodigious event, of incalculable importance, without which the whole future of Christianity would have been changed. We may suppose that it impressed the imagination of that age as much as it astounds ours, for the Book of Acts relates it not merely once (in chapter 9), but on two other occasions (chapters 22 and 26), and the two latter by the lips of Paul himself. Basically, the three narratives are absolutely identical; the differences bear only on details: whether Paul's companions also fell to the ground, and just what they perceived—a blinding light or a voice uttering incomprehensible words. The authenticity of the fact is indisputable, and the Apostle was to confirm it on several later occasions by decisive allusions in his letters (1 Cor. 9:1; 15:3; Gal. 1:12, 17). On the road to Damascus, in the midday sun, he found himself face to face with Jesus and heard himself called by name.

He got up from the ground and staggered. Undoubtedly, he cried out; he could no longer see. The text of Acts says he could no longer see "because of the dazzling light." Doctors who have studied this sudden blindness have concluded that it cannot be identified with that caused by sunstroke in the Sahara; the latter is of short duration, while Saul's blindness continued for several days. They have compared it with electric blindness, which is due to excessive light shock on the retina and brings on superficial burns of the cornea and secretions of purulent

mucus; this may last for some time. "One does not see the face
of God without dying," says the Bible. Saul had not died for
having encountered God in this life, but nevertheless it was as
a dead man that he was to resume his journey, a man who had
died to himself. Aided by the men of his escort, he entered
Damascus to await the promised orders.

Damascus was then what it is still, a marvelous oasis,
which seems to rise from the inhuman desert like a paradisiac
flower on the Tree of Life. Its unfailing springs had brought
forth a variety of vegetation: poplars, aspens, and willows bordered the brooklets and watercourses. In the shade of the
palm trees, pomegranates, apricots, and figs ripened in countless gardens. Everywhere, rose and jasmine mingled their
sweet perfume with that of the tuberose. The crossing here of
routes between East and West had made the city one of the
centers where the caravans halted—caravans bound for
Egypt, Mesopotamia, and Persia, carrying furs, silks, salt, or
precious metals. In this powerful city where ten races met, the
long-since numerous Jewish colony (Flavius Josephus speaks
of fifty thousand souls) consisted of well-to-do shopkeepers
and artisans. The city was more or less dependent on the
Arab king, Aretas, who protected it from his distant, rock-
hewn citadel, Petra.

Passing through the fortified gate—it was guarded by a
massive tower—the traveler found himself in an avenue some
fifteen hundred feet long by eighty wide, bordered by porticoes of Corinthian columns, with walks on either side of the
paved thoroughfare. The street was called "Straight"; it still
exists and is known by its ancient title as well as by its modern
name of Souk el-Tawil, the "long bazaar." A Jew by the name
of Judas lived there, who had undoubtedly been given orders
to receive the envoy of the High Priest. We may imagine Saul
seated in some corner of the patio or the shop, silent, lost in
thought, refusing to eat or drink, with his blind eyes open on
the night of the miracle, a miserable captive in the hands of the
One who had so completely conquered him.

It was in the Jewish community, no doubt, that the first nucleus of the Nazarene's followers had developed. This nucleus must not have been insignificant, inasmuch as it attracted the suspicious attention of the religious leaders of Israel. Ananias was a member, described in Acts 9:10 as a "disciple," that is, one of those whom Saul proposed to bring back in chains to Jerusalem. He was, the book says elsewhere (22:12), "an observer of the Law," one of those first followers of Jesus, whose type was still dominant in this very primitive Church: baptized according to the new faith, but still deeply attached to the synagogue and the observances of their race—men who showed themselves all the more Jewish as they became more attentive to the Word of Christ. Good, prudent, moderate, just in his heart and in his life, he was respected and esteemed by all.

Now, Ananias had a vision. The Lord appeared to him and called to him: "Ananias!" He answered as the Bible relates the ancients did in similar circumstances: "Here I am, Lord!" The visitor continued: "Arise and go to the street called Straight and ask at the house of Judas for a man of Tarsus named Saul. For behold, he is praying." Astonished at receiving such an order, the prudent rigorist dared reply: "Lord, I have heard from many about this man, how much evil he has done to thy saints in Jerusalem. And here too he has authority from the high priests to arrest all who invoke thy name." But the mysterious voice resumed: "Go, for this man is a chosen vessel to me" (Acts 9:10–15).

An amazing meeting! This man who feels he is threatened, not only in his person but in his faith and hope, is to go bearing salvation to the very one from whom he may expect the worst. The Christian paradox is here completely formulated, the paradox of Christ's charity, which Saint Paul was to understand so profoundly and to raise to such sublime heights; in the instant when the decisive call was to sound for him, it was necessary that he be affronted. "To love one's enemies, to forgive those who injure us"; Saul was to receive this most essential of all the Gospel lessons from the lips of the very man who, an instant before, had still been his eventual victim.

So Ananias set forth. He entered the house of Judas and asked for Saul. He was there, still prostrate, still blind, still unable to explain what was going on in his soul. "Brother Saul," said Ananias, "the Lord has sent me—Jesus, who appeared to you on your journey—that you may recover your sight and be filled with the Holy Spirit." Instantly there fell from Saul's eyes something like scales and he recovered his sight. He arose and took some food and his strength returned. It was then that he was baptized.

Thus was accomplished what we customarily call "the conversion of Saint Paul." If there were in him secret approaches of grace, unknown even to himself, if there were discernible elements which contributed to the staggering psychological shock on the road to Damascus——all this is of secondary importance. The impression which one draws from reading the Book of Acts, and to which Paul himself obstinately attested all his life long, is that while he still believed himself shot through with Judaist convictions he was caught up in an overwhelming event which changed him completely, at a single stroke. His transformation was radical and complete. What he had hated one day he adored the next. And the cause he had fought so violently he was to serve with the same violence. In a single second on the desert trail God had conquered His adversary and bound him to Him forever.

This man whom the Light struck down upon the road was conquered, but in this defeat his heart's most profound desires had been fulfilled. How can we regard him without emotion, and, we must admit, without a sort of envy? Saul . . . Saul of Tarsus . . . more sinful than ourselves, the executioner whose hands were stained with the blood of the faithful, and who had this inconceivable fortune of meeting Christ personally, of being called by name by His voice. Why was it so? Why was this man pointed out? We find ourselves here in the midst of the Pauline mystery of grace where, in the secret designs of

Providence, all is obscure, and yet wherein all leads to the one goal, which is the deciding Light. It is towards this goal, towards this Light, that Saul shall henceforth tend. The Christ, Who conquered him, will parade him on the highways of the world, as His captive and His slave. As for Saul, he will find the hours of his life always too few to attest adequately his love for the One who had loved him enough to strike him to the heart.

Chapter 2

〜

BY ORDER OF THE
HOLY SPIRIT

Apprenticeship

Was not this man whom Christ had taken the trouble to conquer and to bind to Himself personally, by this very fact, set
apart for an unrivaled destiny, for a particular mission? Paul
was conscious of this from the beginning, and he was to bear
this conviction in his heart throughout his life. Christ had
appeared to him, as true, as real as He had appeared to Peter,
Magdalene, Thomas, and the others during the forty days of
His Resurrection. He had called him by name. Therefore he,
Paul, was an apostle, not in the same way as the Twelve, but
as validly as they; to him alone, among the thousands of saints,
the Church has granted this title. And how often, with legitimate dignity, he was to lay claim to this privilege!

With dignity, but without pride, for he well knew that the
glory did not redound to him. While he often exclaims, "I am
an apostle," to affirm the authenticity of his mission, he adds at
once, with great humility, "I am the least of the apostles, and
am not worthy to be called an apostle, because I persecuted
the Church of God" (1 Cor. 15:9). The merit for the act which
transformed him did not belong to him; but it invested him
with a special character, a unique mission. This God who
"from his mother's womb had set him apart and called him by

His grace, to reveal His Son in him" (Gal. 1:15–16)—had specific intentions for him. He was an apostle, yes, but not for the same purpose as the others. This is the meaning of the declaration which he was to send to his friends in Galatia: "I give you to understand, brethren, that the gospel which was preached by me is not of man. For I did not receive it from man, nor was I taught it; but I received it by a revelation of Jesus Christ" (Gal. 1:11–12). The other apostles had been recruited by the Messiah during His life, as a man chooses and forms those in whom he sees his disciples and spiritual heirs; but it was through an astounding miracle that Paul had been elected.

To learn what Christ expected of him and to prepare himself to accomplish it—this was the immediate obligation faced by Paul after these prodigious events. Could he count on men to enlighten him on what he had to undertake? Apparently he could not; it was a matter between himself and God, between Christ the Conqueror and His conquest. What he had to do, then, was not to consult "flesh and blood" (Gal. 1:16)—and Paul refrained from this—but to place himself in the presence of God and to let His command resound in the depths of his being.

Immediately after his cure he spent a few days with the followers of Christ in Damascus and preached in the synagogues, declaring that Jesus was indeed the Son of God. This struck many with amazement. Those who heard him said: "Is not this he who used to make havoc in Jerusalem of those who called upon this name, and who has come here for the purpose of taking them in bonds to the chief priests?" (Acts 9:19–22). It was undoubtedly advantageous for his testimony to be given in this way, that the glory of the Master might be manifested, and we may presume that it was the judicious Ananias who, for obvious reasons of propaganda and apologetics, requested the object of the miracle to come forth and speak. (One tradition would have it that Ananias was the moral leader of the Christian community of Damascus and at its head died a martyr during the persecution initiated by Lucianus, the Roman prefect of the city.) But Paul soon decided that, for the moment, he had given enough to men, and that it was more important to reflect on the how and why of all this.

Then it was that, as the Epistle to the Galatians briefly indicates (Gal. 1:17), "without taking counsel of flesh and blood," Saul departed for Arabia, that is, for some isolated spot in the Syrian desert of Transjordania, where he could listen to God in silence. Since the time when Moses withdrew into the land of Midian to discover the meaning of his mission and heard the word of Yahweh leap from the midst of a burning bush, all the elect of the One God, all of the prophets, had drawn from such retreats the spiritual energy which was to sustain their undertakings. Consider the retreat into the Djebel Qarantal with which Jesus began His public life; picture John the Baptist fasting and meditating in the terrible wasteland before descending to preach and baptize in the shallows of the Jordan. Great works are born in solitude: the Fathers of the Church, the great founders of orders, have always known and tested this truth.

Paul remained for a long time in Arabia. For about two years he did nothing but pray, meditate, and try to understand. Now that he possessed a golden key that opened all the doors, the Holy Scripture, which he had thought he knew so well, must have shone with new splendors. How difficult it was to reconcile the man he had been, the hard and prideful Pharisee, with the new man who had risen on the road to Damascus, and who resembled him so little! In the gray solitude of the dunes or in the shelter of some cleft in the rocks, nourishing himself with dried figs, locusts, and a sort of white truffle found in the desert—precious as manna—Paul lived for days and days in silence. No, not in silence, for now more than ever there must have sounded in his ears the ineffable voice which the Psalmist says "breaks down the cedars of Lebanon, breaks open the walls, and shatters all solitude," the voice which has no need of words to be heard in the depth of the heart.

Two years flowed by, and, with his foundations well established, Paul had still another task to carry out: his apprenticeship as Christ's conqueror. Paul imposed on himself, so to speak, feeling it an imperious necessity, that novitiate which, in their wisdom, the founders of orders impose on young souls who wish to give themselves to God, that preparation—varying from five to nine years, according to the rules—for the difficult life that will be theirs. Through long years he was to reflect, work, add to his knowledge, test his methods. It was probably in the year 38 or 39 that he came forth from the solitudes of his retreat, weak, weary, exhausted, with burning eyes and bronzed features; he was not to undertake his first mission before the year 45 or 46.

He returned to Damascus, found his friends, and began to preach again. But it seems that during his absence the chiefs of the Jews faithful to the Torah, having recovered from their surprise, had regained their self-confidence; perhaps they had consulted Jerusalem. Paul's preaching in the synagogues met with resistance. The anti-Nazarene movement which he had supported two years before was now turned against him. The oratorical talents and the solid, subtle dialectics of the student of Gamaliel were proving of great advantage in the public debates. The synagogue presidents and the Sanhedrites of Damascus were disturbed by these successes and resolved to put an end to them.

The great Syrian city was then in an ambiguous political position, in principle subject to Rome, but controlled also, in fact, by Aretas, the king of the Nabataean Arabs. It was believed that he welcomed the support of the Jewish colony, perhaps because at the moment a rather active anti-Semitic movement was developing in the Empire; perhaps, too, because the Israelite bankers were already extremely influential. It was to Aretas that the Sanhedrites turned. A delegation went to Petra to ask him to silence the infidel. Orders were given; Arab guards were posted at the city gates to prevent his escape and Jews kept watch near them, to recognize him and point him out. But Paul's disciples were alerted in time and decided that he should escape. It was a delicate and difficult operation, bold and picturesque. In the middle of the night, closed up in one of those enormous baskets used to transport fish, fruit, and vegetables to market, he was let down by a rope over the walls, like a package. This romantic, somewhat ridiculous escape was always a source of humiliation for Paul and he later spoke of it to the Corinthians as one of the unpleasant memories of his life. Nonetheless, he was safe.

In Damascus today there is a corner of the ruined ramparts, red and yellow and bristling with thistle and climbing plants, which still bears the name of "Saint Paul's Wall." There are some Arab houses on the ramparts, with their upper floors overhanging the walls, and having seen them, one readily understands how such an escape was possible. A few steps away, in the Greek cemetery, the relics of Saint George the Abyssinian are venerated under a sort of wooden porch. It is related that he was a soldier of King Aretas and was stationed near the place where the basket reached the ground; he turned his head at the right moment, because he was himself one of Christ's followers, and his lapse of discipline resulted in his being executed. A lamp burns above his tomb, as if guarding the memory of that dark night when the little missionary of the Gentiles departed for his destiny.

Earlier, when the Lord had ordered Ananias to go and find Saul, He had said to him: "I will show him how much he must suffer for my name." This peril was the first lesson, a first sign of the hostility which Paul's message was to awaken along his route. Other examples were to be given to him shortly, and in circumstances where he would never have expected them. Leaving his cramped position in the basket, he arose and set out. Where was he to go? He thought of Jerusalem. Why? From all the evidence because he believed it was necessary henceforth to be in contact with the apostles. If he had not judged it opportune to take this step previously, it was because he considered that, as one called by Christ, he had no need of supplementary instruction nor of a sort of investiture.

Now that he himself had determined his plans, he would go to see Peter and the leaders of the Church out of respect or deference, to establish confidential relations with them. Can it be that he had such high hopes? It was mistrust that greeted him.

We would like to be able to know from our texts of the return trip of this new witness of Christ along the same route which he had followed three years earlier with the rage of the executioner in his heart. We would like to know what he felt when he passed by the place where the Christ had cried out to him in the dazzling light of noon: "Saul, Saul, why do you persecute me?" We would like to know what he thought on seeing the very places which the divine Presence had marked with His impress, the Lake of Tiberias, the Samaritan's Well, the hills where the crowds had gathered to hear Him. And if, as is probable, he returned to the Holy City by the Gate of Benjamin, we wish we knew the heartrending emotion he must have suffered on seeing, a hundred yards away, in a nondescript funereal terrain, the naked hillock where the Cross had been raised.

Lodging undoubtedly with his sister, who lived in Jerusalem, Paul "tried to join the disciples" (Acts 9:26); the expression in the Book of Acts implies that he found obstacles. Since the execution of Stephen and the ill treatment inflicted on the faithful by Saul himself, the Church must have been constantly on the alert. Herod Agrippa I had just received the Palestinian crown at the hands of his friend, the mad and handsome Emperor Caligula, and if he had not yet begun to persecute the Nazarenes, it was known at least that he was scarcely favorable to the sect. And then, those whom Paul succeeded in meeting showed themselves extremely reticent. The memory of the cruel enemy he had been remained with them; could one really believe this story of a miraculous conversion? In short, "they were all afraid of him" (Acts 9:26). And they turned away from him.

This false and utterly unpleasant situation might have been prolonged indefinitely if a generous and perceptive man had not intervened. His name was Barnabas. He was a Levite, originally from Cyprus, who had considerable authority in the young Church because he had been the first to make the fine gesture of giving all his goods to the community. He was esteemed for his virtue, admired for his wisdom. A "Hellenist," that is, a Jew from a Greek city, he belonged to the circle of which Stephen had been the leader, and he must have known Paul for a long time. Perhaps he had met him at Gamaliel's lectures. Beneath the violent temperament of the future rabbi he had discerned an upright and sincere soul; he trusted Paul and offered himself as his sponsor.

Barnabas having confirmed the truth of the miracle at Damascus, and having given his assurance that the convert had already boldly professed his faith in the Syrian city, the matter was settled promptly. Fists unclenched, hearts were opened. Paul "moved freely among them in Jerusalem, acting boldly in the name of the Lord" (Acts 9:28). He made the acquaintance of Peter, with whom he stayed fifteen days (Gal. 1:18). He also met another apostle, James, "the brother of the Lord" (that is, a cousin of Jesus), a man so holy, so pious, that it was said of him that never in his life had he drunk wine nor eaten meat or fish, and that he spent so many hours in prayer that the skin of his knees had become calloused and wrinkled like that of a camel! The other members of the apostolic college were absent from the Holy City at the time, engaged in bringing the Word to Samaria and Judea.

This sojourn in Jerusalem would have been spent in an atmosphere of fraternal confidence if a new incident had not supervened. It is typical of strong characters that they awaken controversy and leave no one indifferent. The Book of Acts says briefly that Paul "spoke and disputed with the Hellenists" and that they "sought to kill him" (Acts 9:29). It is hardly likely that the word here indicates the baptized "Hellenists," who were debating with the "Judaizers," for it is difficult to imagine brethren in Christ reviling each other like this over questions of observance. The "Hellenists" who opposed Paul were more likely Jews who had come from Greek cities but who were still closely attached to the Law of Moses and who saw in the Tarsiote a successor to Stephen. They planned to submit him to the same fate. On learning this, the members of the community advised Paul to vanish. He hesitated, undoubtedly, not wishing to flee from danger, to shirk his duty, but an order from on high compelled him. One day, as he was praying in the temple, Jesus appeared to him and said: "Make haste and go quickly out of Jerusalem, for they will not receive your testimony concerning me!" And as the one-time persecutor bowed his head, confessing that some defiance and opposition appeared reasonable, since everyone might well regard him as treacherous and suspicious, the Lord cut him short, commanding: "Depart, for I will send you far away to the Gentiles" (Acts 22: 17–21).

The decisive order had been given; for the first time the special vocation of Paul was defined. It was not among his compatriots, among those once faithful to the Law, that he was to bear the Word of Christ, but into the midst of the races who were still pagan, who had not benefited from a monotheistic revelation like the Chosen People, who were to leap directly from total ignorance to total truth. Did the future Apostle of the Gentiles understand at once how new was this work to which Christ called him, how bold, how paradoxical? Years were to pass before he decided to give himself to it entirely, and other experiences were to teach him that this was his real destiny.

Fleeing from Jerusalem, he returned to Tarsus, his native city, and stayed there for some time. What did he do there? What results did he obtain? The texts do not tell us, but the impression which emerges is one of a stalemate, of a mediocre success. "No one is a prophet in his own country"; and if the Master Himself painfully proved the truth of the proverb, we may doubt that the disciple was more fortunate. Among his own people, in that Pharisaic background with its rigid discipline and narrow formalism, how alien he must have felt, this man who had tasted the freedom of Christ! How could his kindred understand his marvelous, dramatic adventure on the road to Damascus? And if he ventured to say that his own mission would be to give the message of salvation to those unbelievers of whom the Talmud counseled: "be he the least of the *Goyim*, slay him!" there is no doubt that he would have simply scandalized them. Much later, in the course of his second missionary journey, Paul was to see again the Cilician communities which he had founded during this time; he was to say of them that they had need of being "strengthened" (Acts 15:41); they were poor things undoubtedly, quite small beginnings. Paul was at this stage of his experience, and undoubtedly he was beginning to understand that one does not resist God's orders, when, once more Providence took him by the hand. One day, when he was outside his house, he saw a man come looking for him; it was Barnabas, who had come from Antioch to bring him back there. A new and important step was about to be taken in the future missionary's apprenticeship. In the city of the Orontes he was going to approach the problem of evangelizing the pagans and he was to prepare for it. This was the reason that Barnabas wanted Paul in Antioch.

While Paul had been letting the years slip by in a kind of interior novitiate, the history of Christianity had marched on. The persecution which had followed the murder of the deacon Stephen had driven groups of Nazarenes to flee from Palestine, and some had settled in the Syrian cities, notably Antioch. A community of the faithful had been established there, in which for the first time, baptized natives of Cyprus and Cyrene had dared to speak of Christ and His teachings to the pagans.

Antioch was at that time the cosmopolitan city par excellence, in which all the races of the known world were mingled. The third city of the Empire, after Rome and Alexandria, called "the Beautiful" or "the Golden," she doubly merited these epithets by her natural setting and her wealth. At the foot of Mount Silpius, the color of rust and amber, the plain of the Orontes spread forth its orchards, palm gardens and fields with an inexhaustible luxuriance; the pale green waters of the river washed against the stone arches of the bridges. The four quarters of the city rivaled each other in temples, baths, colonnades, and race courses; there were five miles of streets paved with marble; and business was carried on in Antioch in everything that could be bought or sold. A city of commerce, of luxury, and the theater, Antioch was also the city of all the vices. Juvenal was certainly not wrong when he censured the waters of the Orontes for having sullied those of the austere Tiber. The temple of Daphne alone included in its sumptuous precincts of five hundred acres more than a thousand "priestesses" vowed to the orgiastic cult of the goddess. The saying *Daphnici mores*, "Daphnic morals," was heard throughout the Empire, and everyone knew what it meant. It was in this unlikely city that the good seed of the Gospel had been sown and it had grown there. It had thrived as well among the members of the Jewish colony, who for three centuries had been quite numerous, as among the pagans sympathetic to monotheism, who were known as the "God-fearing." This community of the faithful had assumed such great importance that the entire city knew of its existence; some people were keenly interested in it, some joked about it. Antioch was the home of the humorous remark and the ironical surname; thus, probably in mockery, the name "Christian" had first been given to the disciples of Jesus there. Until then the Jews had called them Nazarenes; among themselves the followers of Christ had used the names *brethren, saints*, or *believers*. In this Christian community of Antioch, Paul worked for about a year under the direction of Barnabas; he preached, he taught, he instructed neophytes, he expounded the mystery of Christ to the congregations. This young Church had great vitality. Its prophets and doctors became more numerous daily, an obvious proof of the gifts of the Holy Spirit. It seemed that, transplanted in this new terrain, the Gospel seedling was growing earnestly in root and branch, and this success was all the more providential since, at that very moment, the mother community, the church of Jerusalem, was undergoing an extremely grave crisis, desolated by famine and ravaged by the persecution which Herod Agrippa II had just launched and which was threatening the life of Peter himself. Moved at receiving such sad news, the Antioch community sent Barnabas and Paul to the Holy City to bring aid in food and money to the brethren. When they returned—bringing with them a young cousin of Barnabas named Mark—the two men announced to their friends in Antioch a great decision. During this charitable visit to Jerusalem they had apparently realized that the future of Christianity no longer lay within the narrow walls of the Holy City, in that threatened community, and the sages who were to direct Christianity in Antioch, Simon the Black, Lucius of Cyrene, Manahem and the others, listened to their plan.

Now once more, the Lord intervened. He had never ceased to concern Himself personally with the one whom He Himself had chosen. At Antioch he had granted him a sublime ecstasy in which, more than to any other mortal man, he had revealed the Secret of the ineffable realities, as Paul was later to report in his Second Epistle to the Corinthians, "I know a man in Christ who . . . was caught up to the third heaven . . . and heard secret words that man may not repeat" (2 Cor. 12: 2, 4). At this moment when everything was at stake for His disciples, how could the Spirit be silent? As the assembled leaders of the Christian community of Antioch prayed and fasted in order to decide wisely on the proposals of the two friends, the Holy Spirit spoke. "Set apart for me Saul and Barnabas unto the work to which I have called them" (Acts 13:2, 3). It was done. The destiny of Saul entered a new phase.

Christ Came for All Men

The work for which Paul had been "set apart" by order of the Holy Spirit was nothing less than the fundamental work of all

Christianity as Christ Himself defined it when, in the last hours of His risen life, He gave to His followers His final precepts: "Go, therefore, and make disciples of all nations, baptizing them in the name of the Father and of the Son and of the Holy Spirit . . . preach the Gospel to every creature. He who believes and is baptized shall be saved" (Matt. 28:19; Mark 16:15, 16). All the exigency of Christianity is in these words, and also, its limitless perspectives; because he understood totally the meaning of this order, the miraculous convert of the road to Damascus was to commit his own life definitively to the decisive way and the Church herself was to enter on her true destiny.

How were these words of Christ to be understood? In two different ways or, rather, with two different accentuations. First of all they contained a general, imperious command, "Go! Preach!" An order which Jesus had repeated all His life long; "men do not light a lamp and put it under a bushel." For a Christian this is his first duty; to brandish this light he has received, to spread and make known the message left with him. Essentially, as well as in his destiny, a follower of Jesus can only be an apologist, a missionary, a conqueror for Christ; it was this compulsion which the Holy Spirit in the course of long reflections and of one of the pathetic confrontations, had placed in the heart of the future Apostle; it was for this task of propaganda that he had prepared himself in the solitude of Hauran as well as by his labors in Antioch; henceforth, throughout his life he was to be marvelously faithful to this injunction: "Woe to me if I do not preach the Gospel!" he was one day to exclaim (1 Cor. 9:16). No man ever answered this vocation better than he did.

But Jesus had made precise the character of His order, its universal character. It is "to all the nations" that the Word is to be brought; it is to "every creature" that the Gospel is to be communicated. The message of Christ takes no account either of political frontiers or of social categories; in His eyes there is "neither Greek, nor Jew, nor circumcised, nor uncircumcised," only brothers, equal before the promise of salvation. Saint Paul was to contribute more than anyone else to formulating this essential nature of Christianity in imperishable terms and to infusing it into the blood and marrow of the Church; it is beyond doubt that this was the subject of the ineffable revelations which he received from the Son and the Spirit, and that this was the culmination of his ten years of meditation.

Concretely, how was Paul to conceive his own mission in the framework of the action he was to undertake? In the sense in which the Lord had revealed it to him in the course of the ecstasy in the temple, that is, as addressing himself to the innumerable peoples who lived in the heart of the shadows, "in the world without God." Had not the prophet Isaiah said, in a formula that Saint Paul was to cite "they to whom it was not told of Him, have seen; and they that heard not, have beheld" (Is. 52:15). Much later, writing to the faithful of the Church at Rome, the Apostle was to say that he always made it a point of honor never to preach the Gospel where the name of Christ had already been pronounced, lest he should build on other men's foundations (Rom. 15:20). The foundations upon which the first Church, the community of Jerusalem, had been built were those of Jewish traditions and Mosaic observances, the solid, hard, rugged bases of the Law. The mission with which Paul knew he was invested was to build elsewhere, on other courses. This is what the Holy Spirit had revealed to him.

In the moment in which he was about to launch out into the great adventures of his missions, Paul certainly saw before him the immense plan in the realization of which he was to consecrate his life, that plan which was later summed up in the same letter to the Romans: to implant the Gospel in every part of the Empire, from Jerusalem to the limits of the West, to call to the light all the peoples of the known world.

The entire future of Christianity was there, in the initiative of genius; both the planting of the mustard seed in the midst of the good ground prepared by Rome, and the Revolution of the Cross overthrowing the established pagan order, and, gradually, the substitution of the man of Christ for the man of the old tradition. This audacious option on the future appears quite natural to us modern Christians, precisely because we think of Christianity in the spiritual light of Saint Paul and because its universality has become our flesh and blood. But we must take account of the audacious character of such a decision, of its disturbing and paradoxical elements: the wise men who directed the Christian community at Antioch had hesitated to accept it and no less than a supernatural order had been required to convince them. This option on the future presupposed the solution of a very delicate problem of the past.

To understand the seriousness of this problem and the terms in which it was then posed, we must anticipate the future and put aside the narrative of Saint Paul's first mission, on which we see him leaving Antioch in the year 46 and setting sail for Cyprus; we must look ahead to the end of this first voyage, in the course of the year 49 and 50. Returning from many adventures in Asia Minor, with the consciousness that they had worked hard for the cause of Christ, and often at the risk of their lives, Paul and Barnabas found the Christians of Antioch in a state of agitation.

Some delegates from Jerusalem had come to the city of the Orontes to reproach the Christians of Antioch for not being faithful to what, according to them, was the true teaching of the Lord. The charge was brought in such a way that it was the apostolate of Paul and Barnabas which was censured and incriminated. The arguments soon reached such a degree of effervescence that the leaders of the Antioch community thought that, to settle the question once and for all, it was desirable to call a meeting in Jerusalem of the authorities of the Church. Paul and Barnabas were therefore sent to the Holy City, together with Titus, a young pagan only recently converted.

What was the point at issue? Exactly this: what was to be the attitude of the Christian Church with regard to the Mosaic Law and Jewish observances? In all certainty it was among the chosen people that Jesus sowed the Word; He formally declared, "I was not sent except to the lost sheep of the House of Israel" (Matt. 15:24), He had even assured that He had not come to destroy the Law or the Prophets, but to fulfill them (Matt. 5:17). In this community of Jerusalem, born at the foot of the temple, some saintly souls, while adhering to the teachings of Jesus, had thought it best not to break with the traditions of their nation but rather, on becoming Christians, to be more profoundly faithful to the God of their fathers and to work more efficaciously for the coming of His kingdom.

But in these circumstances what was happening to the great universalistic idea of Christ, the idea expressed in His celebrated words at the period of the Resurrection? He had given them an example in performing miracles for a pagan centurion and a Phoenician widow and in speaking on friendly terms to an heretical Samaritan woman. To anyone who reflects on the method which Jesus followed, it is clear that He conceived the expansion of His doctrine on two planes: for the faithful Jews it was to be the fulfillment of their traditional religious needs; a second and definitive stage—to the pagans, still in darkness, it was to bring the light at once. But the Judaizing Christians, the members of the community at Jerusalem, were to be excused if they understood the first aspect of this teaching better than the second, and if they were convinced that it was to them, and to them alone that the promises belonged.

However, a broadening tendency had developed even in this narrow Judeo-Christian milieu, and here again the Holy Spirit intervened. Peter, the Prince of the Apostles, the old rock on which it had been announced the Church would be founded and who was himself a strict Jew, very faithful to the observance of the Torah, had been obliged by God Himself to confer the baptism of Christ on a pagan. This had taken place at Joppa, on the seacoast; during an ecstasy, he had received the order not to take account of the Jewish prescriptions and prohibitions, and to comply with the appeal of a Roman Centurion named Cornelius, garrisoned at Caesarea, asking that Peter come and instruct him in the faith of Christ. And the wise Peter had accepted!

At approximately the same time, on the road to Gaza, Philip, one of the seven deacons, had engaged in conversation with a generous-hearted Ethiopian officer, and having realized that he was worthy of entering the Church, had granted him the grace of the holy water immediately, at the first stream they came to. In Jerusalem, among the Judeo-Christians of strict observance, these events had been regarded as disturbing; it was agreed that these were exceptions, decided by the Holy Spirit Himself. But that Christian baptism of pagans should become a general rule was out of the question. The perspective suddenly changed when Christianity emerged from Jerusalem and spread into many Jewish communities of the Diaspora in which the followers of the Law found themselves in constant contact with pagans. If the latter addressed themselves to the leaders of the Church, asking to be admitted among the baptized, what answer was to be given them? The Judeo-Christians of Jerusalem thought that they should be told: "Unless you be circumcised after the manner of Moses, you cannot be saved" (Acts 15:1) and that if these newcomers did not submit to all the Jewish observances, they should not be accepted as Christians. On the contrary, Paul, Barnabas, and the supporters of universalist tendencies received these pagans gladly, without forcing them to pass through the intermediate stage of Judaism; and their influence was great enough to bring together all the followers of Jesus, without distinction as to origin, in the same liturgical ceremonies, at the communal agapes where they ate and drank, under the consecrated signs of bread and wine, the flesh and blood of Him who died for all men without exception.

Such was the thesis which Paul, going up to Jerusalem with Barnabas and Titus in the fall of the year 49, was to defend against the partisans of a Christianity rigidly attached to the Torah. The move was an important one; the whole future of the Church was at stake. If the Judaizers triumphed,

Christianity would remain a small Jewish sect, for the majority of the pagans would refuse to submit to the Mosaic requirements, especially to circumcision, which was offensive to adults and regarded as humiliating. If Paul's party won out, the future would reveal the entire Greco-Roman world rushing into the open arms of Christ.

It should be remarked that Paul himself was without prejudice in this matter; it was not because of personal interest that he assumed the position in which we find him. Was he not himself a Jew, "a Hebrew the son of a Hebrew"? Did he not pride himself on being more zealous than many of his contemporaries for the traditions of the fathers (Gal. 1:14) and showing himself blameless "as regards the justice of the Law" (Phil. 3:6)? His whole Pharisaic training, even if one takes into account the fact that his master Gamaliel was the most broadminded of all the rabbis, would have tended to influence him in favor of the Judaizers rather than the universalists. But his experience as a "Hellenistic Jew," his contacts with the pagans, and his first missionary efforts made him aware of the real path of the future; his genius recognized it and the Holy Spirit guided him.

Thus in the fall of 49, Paul and Barnabas arrived in Jerusalem; they had traversed Phoenicia and Samaria and during their journey had related to many churches the successes of Christ among the pagans, which had occasioned much rejoicing (Acts 15:3). In the Holy City the Apostles and the elders received them sympathetically and had them relate all that God had accomplished through them (Acts 15:4). The conversation with Peter, James, John, and prominent Christians continued in an atmosphere of mutual understanding; the Apostles, "pillars of the Church," gave the right hand of fellowship to Paul and Barnabas in token of perfect confidence (Gal. 2:9). It was agreed among them that the task would be divided in this way: the apostles of Jerusalem would work for the conversion of the circumcised, and the missionaries of Antioch and their friends for that of the pagans.

Suddenly the situation grew tense. Some former Pharisees converted to Christianity became indignant. To accept pagans into the Church! To permit them to ignore the holy Torah, not to impose circumcision on them, the observances listed in the sacred book of Leviticus! Sacrilege! This was indeed *destroying* the Law and not *fulfilling* it. It was disobeying Christ Himself! They now came forward with claims and demands. With Barnabas and Paul there had come from Antioch a young Greek by the name of Titus, only recently baptized: let him be circumcised at once! Paul categorically refused to submit his young disciple to this formality; the case of Titus was to be the touchstone. A choice had to be made between Jewish servitude and the freedom of Christ. To put an end to the conflict, the leaders of the Church wisely decided to hold a meeting in which the problem would be thoroughly discussed. It took place in the spring of the year 50; it has often been called— with some emphasis—"The Council of Jerusalem," the first council, which is stretching the meaning of the word somewhat. The partisans and adversaries of Paul expounded their theses, and the debate rapidly turned in favor of universalist Christianity. They had marvelous testimony of what Paul and Barnabas had already done in Antioch, Cyprus, and Asia Minor, in the miracles which God had accomplished through them, and in the conversions that they had made. Peter, who had considerable authority, arose and declared that before God there was no difference between pagans and Jews. "From the instant their hearts were cleansed" (Acts 15:9). James, the very pious James, who was renowned throughout Jerusalem for his Mosaic observances and his lengthy prayer in the temple, spoke in the same tenor. "My judgment," he said, "is not to disquiet those who from among the Gentiles are turning to the Lord"; they were to be asked only to abstain from certain practices which might scandalize Christians of Jewish origin, for example, eating food offered to idols. These interventions were decisive: Paul and his friends had won. When they left Jerusalem they took with them the complete approbation of the Church. An "Apostolic decree" was prepared and confided to two special messengers, Jude Barsabbas and Silas, with the intention of informing the Judaizers of the other churches that opposition to Paul's views must henceforth cease (Acts 15:23–29). "The Holy Spirit and we have decided," the document says in a remarkable formula. The final solution was simple: Christians of Jewish origin were to continue to follow the precepts of the old Law, fulfilling it "in the light of Christ"; but the pagans would have no need of passing through the stage of Judaism in order to become Christians.

Such was the problem which Paul had had to solve before being able to launch out freely in his great missionary work; it appears remarkably remote to us today, but for his contemporaries, for these Christians of the first century, it was a matter of capital importance. Undoubtedly, the Apostle of the Nations gave the first striking proof of his inspired genius in clearly understanding the problem and winning acceptance of its solution. What Christ Himself had ordered in the vision of the Temple was henceforth to be the unique commandment of his whole life. With all the force of his being he was to plunge into the limitless perspective he had opened to the Church.

It should not be supposed that there was to be no further opposition. The same problem was to arise on several other occasions and it would be necessary for Paul to use his authority to avoid doctrinal deviations. One of the first incidents took place in Antioch itself. Peter had gone there—perhaps to arrange for a place of refuge in case persecution made Jerusalem untenable—and had, according to the custom of the Christian community of Assyria, agreed to take his meals with all the baptized, whether they were circumcised or not. The fact was important for a pious Jew, for to eat with a pagan was a contamination. His ecstasy at Joppa had taught the Apostle that it was necessary to transcend these alimentary prescriptions. But now he was not making an exception to the Law, but applying a new principle. Some Judaizers who arrived from Jerusalem reproached him for this; he was really going too far!

And Peter, to avoid shocking them or because of a siege of scruples, decided to avoid the society of the pagans and henceforth ate with the circumcised. The other Christians of Jewish origin imitated him, and Barnabas himself, impressed by the example of the Prince of Apostles, did the same (Gal. 2:11, 13). The church of Antioch was quite simply on the point of cutting itself in two!

Then Paul intervened; with a courage heightened by the conviction of being right, he resisted in the face of Peter and the others. In the midst of the community assembly, sensing that the unity of the day before was going to be broken, he dared to speak out. He discreetly recalled to Peter that he himself had admitted full liberty for the converted pagans; why then, by refusing to sit with them in the brotherly agapes, was he affecting to treat them as second-class Christians? Wasn't he exerting a moral pressure on them, as if, without daring to ask them, perhaps without daring to think it himself, he was expecting them to have themselves circumcised? There was a serious incoherence in this and a grave peril for the Church; we may suppose that the Prince of the Apostles realized this and took the right road.

But the propaganda of the Judeo-Christians was not yet to accept defeat. Paul was to come into conflict with it some years later, at a date which is difficult to ascertain. One of the churches founded by him in the midst of Asia Minor, that of the Galatians, was penetrated by the partisans of Judaist rigorism and exclusivism. Their emissaries came to tell the Christians of Jewish origin that they were contaminating themselves by contact with baptized pagans and that the Gospel preached by Paul was not the true Gospel; in short, they revived the whole controversy. It was necessary for Paul to write them to bring them back to the true conception of things, and his pathetic protest was to afford us the remarkable Epistle to the Galatians in which, brushing away with the sweep of a wing the dust and debris of these wretched questions of circumcision and observances, he put the problem in its proper setting, that of the debate between faith and the rigid disciplines of the Law, that is, between the spirit and the letter; he proclaimed the freedom of the children of Christ, redeemed by His love.

It is the destiny of men of genius to be constantly in conflict with misunderstanding, routine, and human mediocrity; but is their privilege to find in the obstacles placed in their path the opportunity for surpassing themselves, for becoming still more effective, still more courageous.

The Messenger of the Holy Spirit

Let us consider the missionary of Christ, the messenger of the Holy Spirit, at the time when (probably in the fall of the year 46) he is proceeding from Antioch to Seleucia, the great port of the Orontes, there to take ship and begin his great adventure. He is about 40 years old, the age at which we know more or less what we are and why we exist. He himself had defined the meaning of his life and his actions long before he had been led to justify them in the eyes of others at the Assembly in Jerusalem. What manner of man is he to enter on such a path, to assume such responsibility, to bring Christ to the world? What is there in this little Tarsiote Jew that makes him take such a tremendous gamble? Not much probably, in the eyes of men, but He who had chosen him from among all men knew that from all eternity, Providence had conceived, formed, and prepared him for this task and this risk. If the Fisherman had chosen extraordinary means, strong lines, to capture him, it was because He was not unaware of what a great fish He was going to catch.

Undoubtedly, Paul was not conspicuous for his physical bearing, his beauty, or his strength. In any case it is more than likely that the artistic representations of sculpture and painting which show him as a sort of athlete of Christ, a warrior armed with a sword, or a vigorous preacher with a florid face, are excessively idealized and deceptive. The impression received when one reads the texts and tries to imagine the Apostle of the Nations is quite different.

We must admit, however, that it is only an impression. In following closely the Book of Acts and the Epistles, it is completely impossible to determine precisely the physical characteristics and features of the Tarsiote. Even the celebrated incident of his escape in a basket over the walls of Damascus (2 Cor. 11:33) is scarcely informative, and in any event it does not permit us to conclude that he was of extremely short stature; for, on one hand, it is quite possible to be let down in a basket by simply assuming a crouching position; on the other hand, the provision baskets existed in all sizes and some of them were immense, like that mentioned in the Talmud, which held enough bread for a hundred meals! Nor is the fact that his Latin name of Paul suggests the idea of littleness any reason for believing he was short in stature; it is not likely that in Rome all the Pauli were short! And as for the incident which took place at Lystra, during the first mission, when the pagans of the place called Barnabas "Zeus," and Paul "Hermes," we may only conclude that the Tarsiote was less tall and majestic than his companion, and that he was more talkative.

In fact, it is not through Scriptural documents that we are able to form a picture of Paul, but through traditions (impossible to verify, moreover), the oldest of which go back to the last third of the second century, traditions often mingled with elements which are more than suspect but which, nevertheless, as far as they concern Saint Paul are remarkable for their tenacity. It seems that in the primitive Church a description of the Apostle was transmitted from place to place and from generation to generation. Perhaps it originated in a kind of passport which the missionaries carried with them in order to be recognized in the Christian communities which were supposed to receive them—thus a Greek apocryphal text called the Acts of Paul, which belongs to the legend of Thecla and which great Christian writers like Tertullian were to cite freely, gives us this quite unflattering description of the Apostle of the Nations: "of medium height, stocky, bandy-legged, bald-headed, joined eyebrows, a bulging nose"; the sketch is characteristic and requires no commentary. It is true that the anonymous author adds that "his appearance was full of grace and sometimes he looked like an angel rather than a man," whence we may conclude that this little inconspicuous Jew radiated an unquestionable spiritual force.

On the whole all the subsequent documents that have been gathered corroborate this portrait. A writing falsely attributed to Saint John Chrysostom speaks of Paul as a man "Three cubits high (four feet eight inches) who reached beyond the heavens." The famous medal of the Catacombs of Domitilla, which pictures Peter and Paul and which may be seen in the Christian museum of the Vatican, gives the Apostle of the Gentiles a very pronounced Hebraic profile; it is true that its date is questioned and that many believe it is a forgery. A sixth-century text, the *Prince of the Apostles*, by John Malala, adds this detail: gray eyes and heavy beard. A man of small stature, with a large nose, with sparse red hair, a well-formed chin and gray eyes under thick, joined eyebrows: in spite of the majesty which we seem to recognize in him, was this what God has chosen from among all men to be His witness and His spokesman? The choice would be more understandable if he had been a great orator, one of those giants of the Word who with a torrent of molten metal sweep up the deep and confused emotions of their listeners to the point where one forgets physical appearance, and even forgets to examine their arguments; but this was not Paul's type; he acknowledged himself "rude in speech" (2 Cor. 11:6). It goes without saying that, for us, he is much more than an orator, that in the occasional violence of his periods, in the sometime confusing development of his ideas, we see something more than an art or technique: the outpouring of the spirit. But it is quite certain that he had nothing in common with those great rhetoricians of antiquity—an Isocrates, for example—who polished and repolished their style for years, until they came to forget completely the substance and spoke merely for the sake of speaking. What Paul says is what he sees, what he experiences in the rending of his soul; and in his eyes, thought counts much more than style. It is easy to imagine him speaking Greek with a nasal tone, a pronounced Jewish accent, and many provincial expressions, making the refined intellectuals of Athens snort with laughter. It was not with this eloquence that his prestige was to be established.

To complete this utterly inglorious portrait, we must add that Paul was a sick man, that he may have been ill since birth, that, in any case, he became ill in the course of one of his voyages, and that illness was never absent from his preoccupations. It is certain that it did not prevent him from journeying the world over with extraordinary energy nor from accomplishing a work of exceptional magnitude; but is it not commonly observed that achievements which surpass the average are often the work of men in ill health, of failing physical vigor, as if intense spiritual vitality were closely related to some mysterious frailty?

Paul speaks several times of his illness. For example, writing to his Galatian friends, he thanks them for having received him without disdain or disgust when he visited them while seriously ill (Gal. 4:13, 14). And again he mentions to the Corinthians that "thorn for the flesh" (2 Cor. 12:7) which the messenger of Satan plunged into his body to prevent him from becoming proud. One gets the impression that it was a disease so serious and chronic that it could not be forgotten, and painful and conspicuous enough to be embarrassing. What illness was it? A hundred commentators have developed hypotheses, none of which is too convincing: they speak of rheumatism, purulent ophthalmia, intestinal ailments, hemorrhoids, sciatica, leprosy, swamp fever, and, of course, of epilepsy and nervous diseases. The variety of these suppositions is enough to show how groundless they are. One thing is certain, that Paul was ill, knew himself to be ill, and that in his own eyes his illness appeared to be a weakness. This stroke completes the portrait of this unprepossessing man, through whom, however, God was to accomplish such great things. In truth, to judge from appearances, we must conclude that in this case, as always, "how incomprehensible are His judgments and how unsearchable His way!" But beneath this unpretentious exterior, in this intimately wounded and painful flesh, the Creator had placed a soul of unique quality, together with exceptional character. If Paul's physical appearance scarcely arouses enthusiasm, we are all the more impressed by his moral virtues, the spiritual vigor to which his whole life attests and which makes of him an imperishable figure.

What strikes us first and above all is his extraordinary fortitude, his amazing energy. It appears to be inexhaustible. This sick man, who had to consider the demands and limitations of his body, was to travel thousands of miles, more than three thousand on foot and almost ten thousand aboard ship, under conditions in which there was a notable lack of comfort. Nothing in nature checked or discouraged him, nor anything that man could do. It might be said that he was genuinely at ease amid difficulties, tension, and conflict. His worst trials furnish opportunities for greater accomplishments. He speaks of them with an unfeigned serenity. "We are sore pressed, but we are not destitute. We endure persecution, but we are not forsaken; we are cast down, but we do not perish," he declares tranquilly, and this testimony of his is profoundly true (2 Cor. 4:8–9). Never did he weaken, never did he capitulate. That very violence which he had formerly devoted to the service of Christ's enemies henceforth sustains and animates his Christian soul. A figure in every way admirable; few men convey such a striking impression of self-mastery.

What is, perhaps, still more interesting and exemplary in this figure is that his success and achievement do not seem to have come naturally. There are men who march straight forward through life and without hesitation, because they are so constituted that their conscience never poses any problem, because they are ignorant of the abysses along the way. Saint

Paul gives exactly the opposite impression. His famous confession, "I do not do the good that I wish, but the evil that I do not wish, that I perform" (Rom. 7:19), is that of a man for whom a secret drama exists, who has known temptation and conquered it, who has viewed abysmal depths but has not fallen. A being of contrasts, at once tender and demanding, violent and sensitive, energetic and meditative: we may imagine at what cost, through what efforts of self-domination, he was able to achieve unity within himself. If he were merely a forceful man, fully engaged in action, we would admire him as one of those sublime exceptions which nature sometimes makes to the law of human weakness. But when we read him attentively, how much closer he seems to us, how much more brotherly! There is one point in which we may be able to discern his effort at self-mastery; it is the point of the moral life on which so many consciences stumble and fall, that of the flesh and its temptations. In the case of the most glorious of human figures, of the only model, of Christ, we have the certitude that this problem never arose, and that everything in that adorable image breathes forth "nettezza," that absolute purity of which Saint Catherine of Genoa speaks: where Paul is concerned, however, we have the feeling that the drama of the flesh was significant. "I see another law in my members, warring against the law of my mind and making me prisoner to the law of sin": so he declares in the Epistle to the Romans (7:23). But he passed and surmounted this drama; he overcame this law of the flesh. We cannot say precisely whether he married at eighteen, as Jewish law desired (and as Clement of Alexandria assures us), nor whether he was soon widowed; but one thing is certain to anyone who reads the remarkable seventh chapter of the First Epistle of the Corinthians: it is that the man capable of attaining this serenity, this exaltation, a soul who has escaped the slavery of the flesh, our woeful human servitude, and, without having in any way forgotten the demands and weaknesses of our nature, has attained a higher level of the moral life.

Tenacity, discipline, self-mastery—these are the words which constantly come to mind when one thinks of the Apostle of the Nations. But we would be omitting from his portrait some of his most important gifts if we neglected certain traits of his which are infinitely more touching. This man who, all his life long, was involved in excitement and adventure was often to prove himself keenly sensitive. How many men loved him to the extent of linking their destiny with his— proof that he knew how to win affection! The power which radiates from Saint Paul is the power of love; it is not only all humanity, considered abstractly, which he loves and wishes to lead to salvation, but it is each man personally, for love knows only persons, individual beings, each of whom expects to be loved for himself. Thus Saint Paul will tell the Thessalonians that he felt for each of them as a father for his children (1 Thess. 2:11, 12); and will tell the Galatians that, when he thinks of them he is like a mother who has borne a child in her womb (Gal. 4:19). How concerned he is with the care of these Christian communities born of his work, interested, even when he is far away from them, in the slightest details of their existence. He is so often represented as violent, terrible, unbending, fanatically devoted to an austere cause; yet what did he do when he was imprisoned at Rome, in danger of death and would have had plenty of excuses for thinking only of himself? He wrote to his former disciple Philomen, a Colossian Christian, asking him, with great delicacy, to pardon a fugitive slave, Onesimus, and to receive him as a brother. No, the famous passages in which Saint Paul has exalted the all-powerfulness of love are for him not developments of moral theology; he has put into practice these precepts of the charity of Christ; he has lived them.

It is not enough merely to enumerate the moral riches of a nature like Paul's. With Paul, character is intimately associated with intellectual and spiritual gifts, which make of him a peerless being. To remain on the purely human level, the Tarsiote is a genius, and no one who has studied him has been able to escape his magnetism, even those who, like Renan, have hated him and in many respects have misunderstood him. First of all, he had the genius's dazzling understanding of great problems, the gift of going straight to the essential, of not letting himself be stopped by appearances or contingencies; there is something of the eagle's flight in the procedure of a genius; he hangs poised, seeks out his prey, and having found it falls upon it in one swoop. Thus it is with Saint Paul: whether it is a matter of important problems of the past, such as we have seen in his choice between fidelity to the letter and freedom according to the Spirit, or whether it concerns options on the future, such as we shall see him take with regard to Greek philosophy or Roman order, an infallible instinct always guides him, and he decides always in the same way what will be most fruitful to the cause he serves, the richest in prospects for the future.

But he also has the genius's long patience, firmness, and obstinacy. For one of our worst errors is to imagine that great works—works of the mind as well as feats of action—are achieved through chance, by a sort of miracle incessantly repeated. A great work is always, and perhaps above all, a constant effort; a clear and organized intention to which a man seeks to be permanently faithful. On this point again, so many of our accepted opinions give an inaccurate picture of the great Apostle; we see in him only the pioneer who, swept along by the wind of the Holy Spirit, sows the good seed here and there with scarcely any concern as to how it shall grow. Nothing could be more false. Everything indicates that when Saint Paul set out on his long adventures, he had a well-defined plan which took into account requirements and exigencies of time and place, and when he lapses (for example, when an attack of illness keeps him among the Galatians longer than he had foreseen), he carefully notes this exception and takes account of it. As for the meticulous way with which he followed up his work and kept in contact with his "daughters," the communities he had created, one needs only to read any one of his letters to be convinced and to admire him for it.

A dear understanding of the goal to be attained and patient energy in pursuing it: these two constituent gifts of genius are completed by one that awakens and directs them, the spirit of enthusiasm, faith. No great work is realized without this virtue. It goes without saying that, deprived of the other two, it can result in the worst errors and the most tragic failures; but it is still more certain that the being in whom it does not exist is condemned in advance to modest tasks, to minor enterprises, and that great creative ventures are closed to him. One needs a kind of ignorance, almost naiveness, to dare to enter into certain adventures in which, in effect, everything seems to forecast defeat; perhaps it helps to have kept the childish heart—Paul bears within him this superabundant gift. He knows so well how to be mocking and ironical; he is never deceived, either by himself or others; yet, when it is a matter of what, in his eyes, counts more than all the rest, with what confidence and abandon he pursues it! Everything in his nature bears him forward and compels him: his natural impetuousness as well as his desire for sacrifice, his pride, his dominating nature, his instinctive need of commanding and leading men as much as his zeal and his inexhaustible charity. It is his "élan vital," as Bergson says, which leads him to do what he does—extraordinary, superhuman things; such as he is, he could not act otherwise.

Thus, it is little enough to say that he was completely devoted to his work: for him, to live, act, think, or write was exactly the same thing. What we call "his doctrine" is, in reality, only the projection of his personal experience as circumstances have led him to live it. There is not a theology of Saint Paul, a morality or a metaphysics of Saint Paul which exist isolated from the personality of the Apostle and the conditions in which he developed them. There is no *paulinism* in the sense in which we say that there is a *kantism* or a *bergsonism*. There is a man, a genius, who reacts to specific circumstances presented by the event, who reacts to them with all the talents and forces of an extraordinarily rich nature but whose thought is so congenial, so marvelously coherent that it appears to follow some theoretical or prearranged order.

And it is at this point, without doubt, that we must render to Caesar what is Caesar's and to God what is God's. If all the features constituting this genius were fused in this exceptional success, if all the contradictory traits were harmonized in this man, we cannot doubt that there was someone who was there, directing and controlling all and from whom all this mysterious synthesis proceeded: He who, one fine summer day, on the road to Damascus, had risen in the ecstasy of noon and had captured this destiny. Saint Paul is an intellectual genius, a hero of character, but he is not only that, and he is not that primarily. What counts most of all is the spiritual élan within him; it is the action of God, ever present and discernable in all the stages of His existence. If his whole nature gives so strong an impression of unity and rectitude, it is because at one stroke, he surrendered his fate to Him from Whom all proceeds and Who knows the why and the wherefore of all things.

A psychological portrait of the Apostle of the Nations would be meaningless if one forgot that, above all else, he was a mystic, a soul given up completely to God and who maintained with the ineffable Power the perpetual dialogue of a sublime communion. To tell the whole story in one word, if Paul is what he is, if he is to do what we shall see him do, it is because another, who knows him better than he knows himself, is guiding him along his way. Did not the little Jew of Tarsus himself give us the key to his mystery, that day when he cried out magnificently "it is not I who live, but Christ who lives in me"?

Chapter 3

THE GREAT ADVENTURES

"IN MANY MORE LABORS, in prisons more frequently, in lashes above measure, often exposed to death. From the Jews five times I received forty lashes less one. Thrice I was scourged, once I was stoned, thrice I suffered shipwreck, a night and a day I was adrift on the sea; in journeyings often, in perils from floods, in perils from the Gentiles, in perils in the city, in perils in the wilderness, in perils in the sea, in perils from false brethren; in labor and hardships, in many sleepless nights, in hunger and thirst, in fastings often, in cold and nakedness. Besides these outer things, there is my daily pressing anxiety, the care of all the churches" (2 Cor. 11:23–28).

Thus, in a celebrated passage of the second letter to the Corinthians, so beautiful and touching that the great humanist Erasmus justly compared it with Demosthenes, Saint Paul portrayed what his life was through all the time of his missions, that is, for twenty-two years! Yes, for twenty-two long years the ailing missionary was to be constantly on the road, going from city to city, from one Jewish quarter to another, on unsafe roads, on perilous seas, ill fed, working to earn his bread. Many a time he was to meet with distrust and churlishness from the local Sanhedrites faithful to the Torah, who regarded him as a heretic; often too, pagans were to take offense and denounce him to the authorities. He was to be frequently arrested, cast out, a jail bird and fair prey for the police, and none of this was to deter him!

We do not know if there ever existed in history a man who was so devoted to a cause and who gave himself so fully to the service of an idea. The reason for this is that he makes no distinction between his life and his doctrine; both are fulfilled in a unique expression: the more he suffers, the more ills he bears, the closer he approaches the Only Model. A soldier of Christ, a militant of the Revolution of the Cross, he saw the triumph of his cause as his only goal. But could this triumph be surely won in any other way than how the Master Himself achieved victory, through suffering and death? It was specifically with regard to the sufferings borne during his missions that Saint Paul wrote the moving words: "what is lacking of the sufferings of Christ I fill up in my flesh" (Col. 1:24). This tells the whole story.

Thus is explained the Apostle's perpetual joy, the enthusiasm he was to show even in the midst of his worst tribulations. When a believer really understands this sort of game of loser-take-all which is the Christian's destiny, when he knows and experiences to the depth of his being that every trial is a chance for Christ, and that every defeat on the terrestrial level is a victory on another plane, how can he be sad and discouraged? When, while a captive in Rome and in danger of death, the Apostle wrote a last letter to the Philippians, probably the most beloved of all his disciples, what did he tell them: "rejoice in the Lord always; again I say, rejoice. To write you the same things indeed is not irksome to me" (Phil. 3:1). It is all this, this fervor and enthusiasm as well as his intrepid steadfastness, that we must keep in mind as we follow Saint Paul's steps through his great adventures; this revolutionary bears a halo of light, the heart of this terrible wrangler is full of joy.

Concretely, how are things to go for the spokesman of Christ? Let us attempt to sketch the scenario of one of his stops, of one of his missions; pretty much the same details will be repeated wherever he goes. When he arrives in the city for the first time, where does he go? Undoubtedly, to one or another of the quarters where the brethren of his race live; there were Jewish colonies in all the provinces of the Empire, in Asia Minor as well as Syria, in Macedonia as in Greece, and also in Rome. Had not Seneca, who bore them no love, recently written: "the morals and customs of this rascally race are established in every country"? This dissemination of Israel, this Diaspora, was to have a capital importance for the sowing of the Gospel: it is one of those points on which, as Peguy said so well, history, providentially, seems to have been working for a long time on behalf of Christ.

The missionary, then, presents himself to the leaders of the Jewish community. He has with him a kind of passport which accredits him, some letters of recommendation, and is at once fraternally received, according to the law of Moses: as a guest is he not a messenger of Yahweh? If his stay is to be brief he will receive generous hospitality; if he must stop for some time, they will aid him in finding work. For Saint Paul, the latter is usually the case. Hardly disembarked, he seeks employment in a large shop where he will work with his hands at the trade of weaving and tent making which he learned from his father. He wishes to owe nothing to anyone; he wants to be free; he wants also to give an example, for he himself wrote the famous phrase—one which Lenin was to pick up, without citing the source—"if any man will not work, neither let him eat!" (2 Thess. 3:10). He was to be justly proud of this freedom which his work procured for him: "neither did we eat any man's bread at his cost," he said to the Thessalonians (2 Thess. 3:8) and the Ephesians: "these hands of mine have provided for my needs!" (Acts 20:34).

This manual worker, side by side with slaves, plied his shuttle at the loom or tailored coats for the caravan workers. He ingratiated himself quickly, for some peculiar force emanated from him. It was not only with the little people, the proletarians, that he won prestige. The important people seemed to have had respect for him: the proconsul of Cyprus, the Asiarchs of Ephesus, and even the intellectuals of Athens never refused to listen to him; even when he was arrested in Jerusalem, the Roman magistrates treated him with respect; King Herod Agrippa and his sister, Racine's famous Berenice, took pains to see and hear him.

Where did he begin to preach? In the synagogues, those houses of prayer and doctrine, which each Jewish community, almost at the instant of its founding, made haste to construct and in which its meetings were held. Excellent ground for sowing the first handful of the good seed! Actually, one found in the synagogues not only all the faithful of the Old Law, among whom were many sincere and pious souls, full of good will, but also a number of converts from paganism, proselytes who had accepted circumcision, God-fearing men who lived according to the Divine Law, religious-minded men who found no more satisfaction in the state religion than in the mysteries of Isis or Mithra, and who were seeking the monotheistic revelation among the chosen people.

The first Sabbath day after their arrival, Paul and his companions would take part in the ceremonies at the synagogue. Following customs, as strangers, they were asked to speak to the community. This was their opportunity! They spoke. They told of Christ Jesus, His life, His testimony; they described His death and His resurrection: we may still read, in the Book of Acts, the résumé of the speech which Paul made to the Jewish community at Pisidian Antioch (13:16–41); it is simple and moving. At first, the missionaries of Christ were heard with sympathy, but quite soon the Sanhedrite leaders became aware that the doctrine taught by the newcomers ran counter to their traditions; perhaps, too, they received information from other communities. Hostility broke out when the first conversions to Christianity took place; the missionaries of the Crucified were driven from the synagogue.

Paul did not accept defeat. In the meantime he had come to know the city in which they are staying and had made some contacts there. Now he went to preach to the pagans. Where and how? That depended on circumstances and local customs; in a private house or a public square—anywhere at all. His first converts from Judaism assisted him. What did he say to the pagans? Not exactly the same things as he had told the Jews; two of his speeches are summed up in the Book of Acts, those of Lystra (14:15–17) and Athens (17:22–31); they show clearly that Paul sought to adapt himself to his audience, to their prejudices and ways of speech. Thus the first Christian nucleus, which had come from the synagogue, would be augmented by another group of recruits, drawn from among the pagans; all were united fraternally in the same community. Thus churches were born at Pisidian Antioch, Iconium, Lystra, Thessalonica, and Corinth; when the local authorities, alerted by the Jewish leaders or pagan priests, decided to take measures against the nonconformists, the work was done: the seed had been sown in the earth; and it was to grow!

A question arises. On what basis were these cities chosen, these missionary stations, these cities where the seed of truth was sown? However little we know of Saint Paul and his creative genius, it seems inadmissible that this would have been done haphazardly. If, as we have seen, he probably had a general plan of evangelization, he must have marked out in advance a certain number of key positions in which he would solidly establish Christianity, making them points of departure for new conquests. In the course of his missions, he was undoubtedly forced to submit to circumstances; for example, it seems that his stay among the Galatians was prolonged involuntarily, because he was ill. In other cases, however, if he made stays of several months it was because of the importance he saw in the cities' position: Pisidian Antioch, for example, that crossroads of the routes from Anatolia; or Athens, of obvious importance; or Corinth, the great port whose influence radiates across two seas; or Ephesus, a broad gateway opening on Asia. If the Holy Spirit sometimes intervened to guide him—when he hesitated to make a decision personally for example—and if it was a supernatural vision which launched him on his great adventure in Europe, it merely confirms this certainty: in what Paul was to undertake, nothing was left to improvisation.

Here we must recall the circumstances in which the future missionary had been born and had grown up and been educated. What is he? A Jew, the son of a Hellenistic city. This means that he shared in three forms of civilization, that he was traversed by three different currents. We already know what he owes to his Jewish loyalties, and these were the foundations of his strong personality. But because he is a native of Tarsus and a Roman citizen, he has escaped the narrow view of the strict Jewish observance; his eyes are opened on broader horizons. He knows what Europe represents and he knows his orders, his discipline, and the practical universality which presides over his designs. He knows, too, the world of the eastern Mediterranean, that extremely cultured society (with all the good and evil connotations that the term suggests) which has prevailed since those glorious days when Alexander the Great dreamed of gathering the whole world under a single rule. He knows, too, the mechanism and the solid realities as well as the faults and problems of the Greco-Roman society in which he is to work. This was to serve him well.

The field of his activity is the Empire, then at the height of its power. The reign of Augustus, who died in the year 14, opened the golden age of the ancient world. The universe dominated by the sons of the Wolf extends from the Atlantic to the Caucasus, from the Rhine to the upper Nile, with an area of almost two million square miles, and a population of some sixty million. After the checks and disturbances of the final years of the Republic, order was so firmly established that Pliny could justly sing of the "Roman peace." Civil wars are no more; foreign wars, limited to the frontiers and involving only contingents of mercenaries, in no way disturb the mass of the population. Minor political outbreaks were of interest only to a limited circle: the court, the senate, and the bureaucrats; if the madly suspicious Tiberius sends an order for the death of some patrician, or if an uprising in the year 41 puts an end to the crazy reign of Caligula, what does it matter to the citizen of Milan, Bordeaux, or Athens? What matters is that peace is secured, that people can travel on excellent roads without fear of bandits, and that the pirates driven out by Pompey and his successors will not return. This Empire in which one can travel freely without a passport, without changing currency or language, is an excellent ground for spreading a doctrine; the fact must have already been remarked by the first Christians: the *Pax Romana*, too, made for the success of the Gospel.

No doubt, we should not exaggerate these advantages; they were real and appreciable, but one had still to face hardships and danger. Since Paul's destiny was to travel incessantly, how should we picture the conditions in which one traveled in those days? The best way to travel was by sea; protected by the imperial ships of war, an enormous merchant fleet maintained regular lines of service in the Mediterranean. The ships were what would be called today mixed cargo, carrying both merchandise and passengers. The latter might be quite numerous; thus Flavius Josephus speaks of having embarked on a ship carrying 600 passengers. The comfort of these ancient ships of passage hardly resembled that afforded by the ships of our day. Almost all the travelers were crowded together on the bridge and fed themselves as best they could. Moreover, the length of the crossings was extremely variable, depending on the wind, the state of the sea, and visibility conditions. Most of the time the captains preferred to remain within sight of the coast rather than to sail directly across the open sea, even though this considerably lengthened the journey, and there was no navigation at night and during the winter months. Obviously, all this tended to make service irregular.

On land, journeys were more regular but were still slower. There was, indeed, a wonderful network of Roman highways. In Asia Minor, on the high road from Troas to Pergamum, Sardis and Philadelphia, the main road was joined at Laodicea by the route to Ephesus; and then, farther on, by that of Attalia in Pamphylia and of Pisidian Antioch, leading to the Cilician Gates and Tarsus. In Macedonia, the famous Egnatian Way served the whole country, from Dyrrachium to Neapolis and from the Adriatic to the Aegean, passing through Pella, Thessalonica, and Amphipolis and connecting at one end with Byzantium and at the other with many fine Greek roads. All these highways were broad, paved, and well kept up. Along them could be found not only guard houses but a kind of hotel—the caravansary—and also relays, where one could hire horses. But this presupposes a lot of money, and when one was a beggar, as Paul and his companions were, he had to travel on foot along these interminable roads which cut straight across the countryside, climbing and descending hills, and the daily stages never exceeded seven or eight leagues—about eighteen miles!

One conclusion is obvious: the Roman Empire certainly—and unwittingly—favored the missionary work of Saint Paul, assuring him of order, police protection, well-maintained roads and regular ship sailings; nevertheless, twenty-two years of traveling in such conditions could certainly not be considered a pleasure cruise; it required a daily effort effected with energy and fervor.

The Roman world was not only the physical framework in which the Apostle was to pursue his great adventures, but also provided the spiritual and moral climate in which he was to act. What was this climate in the first century, when Saint Paul went forth to cultivate with the keen blade of the plow of Christ? Where so vast a human entity is involved, we must guard against simplifying generalizations. The places and social groups in which the missionary was to work were too numerous for us to attempt to find any homogeneity in them; a savage village of Lycaonia obviously bears little resemblance to the intellectual quarters of Athens, or to the somewhat peculiar fauna of the slums of Corinth! There were still profound differences between Rome and Italy (where the latter part of his life and work were accomplished, regions which were only beginning to be reached by the process which in the course of the following centuries was to lead the Empire to its death), and the eastern areas (where he was to spend three-fourths of his career, that Hellenistic world where, for more than three centuries, heterogeneous elements from Ninevah, Babylon, Persia, and Egypt had been mingled in the Greek melting pot amid social crises, waves of immorality, and religious unrest). It was a land of degeneration which produced both pure and poisonous flowers, Cleopatra and the Venus de Milo. In spite of these differences, this ancient world had a general character which has often been noted and which it would be futile to discuss here: it was a false, illusory structure, secretly menaced in spite of its appearance of equilibrium, a civilization which was socially unjust and which was breaking up morally, which was cut off from its spiritual roots; in short, a world whose whole foundation was about to shift.

Saint Paul profoundly understood this drama of the ancient world. Everything that has been written, or could be written, on moral crises gives way before the astounding pages of the Epistle to the Romans, in which he shows how the spiritual treason of the pagans, their willful blindness, ended in their moral disintegration: "professing to be wise, they have become fools and they have changed the glory of the incorruptible God for an image made like to corruptible man . . . therefore God has given them up in the lustful desires of their heart to uncleanness, so that they dishonor their own bodies among themselves—they who exchanged the truth of God for a lie, and worshiped and served the creature rather than the creator . . . for this cause God has given them up to shameful lusts . . . so that they do what is not fitting, being filled with all iniquity, malice, immorality, avarice, wickedness . . . detractors hateful to God, irreverent, proud, haughty, plotters of evil; disobedient to parents . . . without affection . . . without mercy" (Rom. 1:22–31). A terrible indictment, the justice of which was to be manifested by history when, in

Rome's decadence, all the vices denounced by Saint Paul were publicly displayed.

The genius of Tarsus also brought to light the spiritual aspects of this drama. He knew the vanity and emptiness of the official religion; he ridiculed it, for example, in that passage of the first letter to the Corinthians in which he speaks ironically of the innumerable divinities of Olympus and of the new lords which devotion to Rome and Augustus had just proposed to the masses (1 Cor. 8:4–6). Neither was he duped by the new forms of religion, in which restless souls and confused minds frenziedly sought a way. Speaking of these pagan mysteries, he said without any equivocation: "of the things that are done by them in secret it is shameful even to speak" (Eph. 5:12). Concerning the fanatical devotees of astrology, he justly observed that they enslaved themselves to "the elements of the world" (Col. 2:8). With regard to the asceticism which was extolled by some supporters of Mithraism and the cult of Isis, he lucidly observed—an ambivalent phenomenon well known to modern psychiatrists—that it masked many equivocal elements and that it was often merely a means, not of dominating, but of flattering the instincts. Addressing this society which bore within it an undeniable religious anguish, Paul declared that what it was suffering from was a great absence, an absence which could be remedied by only one being, one truth, one presence.

It was this being of whom he was to speak, this truth which he was to proclaim, this presence which he was to evoke with an eloquence, persistence, and affection which were equally sublime. To renew the basis of morality and rebuild society, as well as to restore peace to the soul, there is only one means; this means does not consist in obeying legal precepts nor in conforming to rituals; it consists in giving one's self entirely to Him Who is at once the ultimate answer to all questions and the One Model for our conduct in life: He was to be the sole subject of Paul's teaching.

The Gates of Faith Are Opened for Pagans

On the jetty at Seleucia in the autumn of the year 46 the travelers who were boarding the mail packet for Cyprus noticed with some astonishment a group of men dressed in the Jewish fashion who, in the incomprehensible tongue of Israel, with many gestures and blessings, were bidding farewell to three passengers who were as soberly attired as themselves. Of the three, one was short and sickly looking but his face shone with zeal and intelligence; the second, tall and handsome, appeared more reserved; the third, still a young man, obviously took his orders from the two others. The merchants of Antioch, on their way to Cyprus to sell their wood and pelts or to buy copper and perfumes, could hardly have been expected to imagine that these three retiring Jews were setting out to conquer the world and that this instant marked the opening of a great chapter in history.

Why had Paul, Barnabas, and John (still called Mark) chosen the island of Aphrodite as the scene of their first efforts? Because Barnabas was a native of the island; he had been raised in an austere family, a future Levite, promised to the Temple of Yahweh; apparently he had thought it fitting to go to his own people first, to offer them the testimony of his faith in Christ Jesus. After two days and two nights at sea, the travelers on the bridge, wrapped in their Cilician greatcoats, saw the rosy outline of the island rise slowly on the horizon; the gray-eyed dawn suddenly fell away in an explosion of golden light, and green and misty in the arms of the brown hills, the quiet bay of Salamis appeared before them.

Today Cyprus is still a very beautiful island, the largest in the eastern Mediterranean; but, with its area of some five thousand square miles, it is just big enough to prevent one from feeling hemmed in, just small enough to keep one constantly aware of the nearness of the sea. It has been compared to a spread-out doeskin, with Cape Andreas as the tail. In ancient times it was richer than it is today; the goats had not yet devoured its forests, its fields had not been desolated by the Turkish domination, and the mines were being worked, those famous mines from which the yellow metal of Cyprus took the name of *cyprium, cuprum,* or copper, which it still bears. Salamis was the principal port and maintained commerce with the whole Phoenician coast; in the interior was Paphos, the modern Baffo; completely reconstructed by Augustus after a violent earthquake, it was a city of luxury, a little capital where the governor resided.

The entire island was consecrated to Aphrodite, the sea-born goddess, the Anadyomene. The poets tell how Gaea, the earth, having wedded Ouranos, the sky, and having given him many children in the spring, had been outraged when, during the winter, her spouse devoured them all; she had therefore asked her son, Chronos, or Time, to put an end to the frightful habits of his father, and Chronos, with one stroke of his scythe, had emasculated the creator of the gods; falling into the sea, the celestial trophy had shaped a living form on the crest of the waves—the supreme and adorable child of heaven, a ravishingly beautiful woman, a goddess, Aphrodite. It seems that today the high tides sometimes cast on the Cyprian coasts enormous masses of foam that resemble mysterious human shapes. At any rate, two thousand years ago the goddess of love was adored throughout the island; she was represented under the appearance of a sexual organ crudely carved in black stone; on the anniversary of her birth an immense procession, a monstrous phalliphoria, spread out over sixty stadia; and in the evening the young women of Cyprus, as priestesses of the divinity, were supposed to give themselves up to sacred prostitution. For the Apostle's first contact with paganism, it is difficult to imagine a climate more opposed to the purity of Christ, to His morality of respect for women and chastity.

The Jews on the island were numerous. Many had interests in the copper mines, which Herod the Great had turned over to Augustus. Later, in the time of Trajan, when the Israelite revolt broke out all over the Near East, Eusebius says

that two hundred forty thousand pagans were killed by the
Jews on this island alone, proof that the Jews themselves must
have been much more numerous. Barnabas was widely
acquainted at Cyprus, and the three missionaries had hardly
disembarked when they were invited into the synagogues,
where they spoke to their compatriots. But a supreme command led them to change their plans and to make for Paphos.

A Roman possession since the year 58 B.C. and an inde-
pendent province since the year 22 of our era, Cyprus had at
first depended on the Emperor, then had been entrusted to the
Senate, which was represented on the island by a proconsul.
The latter was at that time a patrician of an illustrious family,
Sergius Paulus; he was an intelligent cultured man, on the
model of his predecessor in this post, Cicero, who was himself
the author of a treatise on the customs of Cyprus which was
commended by his contemporary, Pliny. He was one of those
individuals—quite numerous in this era—who were dissatisfied
with the formalism of the official religion and were seeking in
philosophy and in foreign cults for the answer to the great
problems of life. Learning of the arrival in his domain of these
odd people, who were said to be teaching a new doctrine,
Sergius Paulus called them before him.

The meeting of the Roman magistrate and the Apostle of
the Nations was to be of great importance in the destiny of
both; this can be construed even from the stolid account of the
meeting in chapter thirteen of the Book of Acts. The meeting
was marked by a picturesque incident. The group around the
magistrate included one of those specialists in the occult sciences—a magician, astrologist, and other things besides, of a
type which abounded in the society of that time; of Semitic
origin he was named Bar-Jesus, "son of Jesus," but in Greek he
used the name Elymas the Sage. Uneasy at seeing these newcomers breaking down his influence, he attempted to discredit
them with the proconsul.

"But Saul, . . . filled with the Holy Spirit, gazed at him and
said, 'Oh full of all guile and of all deceit, son of the devil,

enemy of all justice, wilt thou not cease to make crooked the straight ways of the Lord? And now, behold, the hand of the Lord is upon thee, and thou shalt be blind, not seeing the sun for a time.' And instantly there fell upon him a mist of darkness, and he groped about for someone to lead him by the hand" (Acts 13: 9–11).

This miracle was to have its consequences. In the first place, Sergius Paulus, deeply impressed, believed in the truth to which Paul had just testified. Did he fully accept Christianity? Did he receive baptism? No doubt, he limited himself to showing sympathy for the new doctrine, for his son and grandson, who subsequently held high posts in the magistracy, do not seem to have belonged to the Church. At all events, he was henceforth the friend and protector of the missionaries—the first fortunate consequence; a pagan of illustrious birth had showed respect for the spokesmen of Christ; this was encouraging.

The other consequences concerned Paul himself. His authority having been strikingly demonstrated, he is now accepted as the leader of the little band; previously he had been the aide of Barnabas; now the Book of Acts will always mention him as the leader, and the apostolic caravan will be designated as "Paul's following"—a decisive reversal of roles, for the genius of Tarsus can now take the initiative and launch out freely on the great enterprises he has conceived. Whether it was to be more at ease in his relations with the pagans or to show his gratitude and friendship to the first high-born Roman who had supported him, from this moment on he definitely abandoned his Israelite name of Saul and always used his Latin name. Saul gave way to Paul, and this is the name we shall see from now on in the Book of Acts. If we consider the importance which the Jews, like all Asians, attached to names, which in their eyes were invested with a kind of supernatural value, we must see in this choice something more than a diplomatic move: it was the manifestation of a spiritual purpose the total acceptance, perhaps, of the very special mission which the

Lord had entrusted to the Tarsiote. At Cyprus Paul learned from experience that the conversion of pagans was possible; he could now enter a broader field of activity.

The new ground where Christianity was to be sowed was Asia Minor, the abrupt, massive plateau, larger than France, which forms an elongated rectangle between the Eastern Mediterranean, the Black Sea, and the Aegean. This region offered few advantages to the bearers of the Gospel. How can the hurried traveler of today, who crosses these monotonous steppes in the sleeping cars of the Anatolia Express, estimate what effort, suffering, and peril were represented in the creeping progress of the missionaries? To cross arduous defiles and snow-covered passes, to march for days on end over desert trails, to bear the extreme shifts of a climate made miserable by four thousand feet of altitude and the oppressive continental influences, to risk frostbite and sunstroke, malaria on the lower plains, Malta fever and other diseases everywhere—all this must have been the least of their troubles, for they had to be constantly on the alert for bandits, who reappeared as soon as one left the Roman guard post behind. In those days Asia Minor was certainly less desolate than it is in our time, when centuries of Turkish neglect have resulted in a tragic regression of culture and communication; but it is certain, too, that all the regions traversed by the missionaries were not equally deserted and that there were great differences between rugged Lycaonia, for example, and Lydia, "rich as Croesus." On the whole, however, it might be considered an amazing venture to launch an attack on such a region in order to teach a message of love and hope.

Lonely shepherds are still to be seen in these regions, wrapped in their *kepeniks*, their large goat-skin capes, so heavy and stiff that they remain standing when the wearers step out of them; they are marvelous protection against the weather of the high plateaus but heavy baggage during the great heats. It is probably in this garb that we must picture Saint Paul and his companions as they traveled along the Anatolian roads; it was perhaps such a cloak which Paul asked Timothy to send to keep him warm in his Roman prison. They walked for days and days to reach the city they had designated in their itinerary. They slept anywhere they could—in a stable, an abandoned khan, often under the open sky; most of the time they ate what they had brought with them—barley bread and dried fish. One needs an iron constitution to withstand such a routine.

As for the people to whom they were to preach, these presented still more difficult problems than the discomforts occasioned by the weather. There was a little of everything in this vast Anatolian peninsula: ancient races deriving from the Carians, the Hittites, and the legendary Trojans; newer elements, Semites from Assyria, Greeks who had arrived since Alexander's time, many Romans, and even some Galatians, near cousins of the Gauls, whom the wanderings of the ancient Aryans had deposited there in the heart of the high plateaus. In all the cities, of course, there were lively, flourishing Jewish colonies, generally in good favor with the local authorities.

A mosaic of peoples! It was a mosaic, too, of cults and beliefs, in which the old totemism and rustic animism served as a base for the mysticisms of Cybele, Dionysius, and Mithra, cults which inclined to violence and fanaticism. It is understandable that in the face of such an undertaking a temperament less steeled than Paul's would have been uneasy and hesitant. So it was with Mark, the young secretary of the Apostle, who had undoubtedly become familiar with his master's character during weeks of traveling together. Mark was faithful and good-hearted; he was to prove that when he wrote his Gospel, and besides, Paul bore him no hard feelings; but in the face of these hardships and perils he gave way and left the little apostolic troop. It is easy to find excuses for him!

The missionaries embarked at Paphos and landed at Attalia, a little port in Pamphylia. The blue harbor, framed by red and yellow cliffs above a semi-circle of wretched white hovels, clings so closely to the steep ascents of the Pisidian hills that it is hard to see how any trail could follow that stairway

to the sky. However, this was Paul's intention. Leaving
Pamphylia to others, who had probably begun working there
already, he intended to head straight for Pisidian Antioch,
where he would find the great Roman highway running from
Troy to the Cilician Gates. About ten stages were planned,
among semi-barbarian peoples, on a miserable second-class
road. At Perge, where Mark deserted, Christ's conquerors
began their attack.

Located at the crossroads of Pisidia, Phrygia, and southern
Galatia, Antioch was one of sixteen cities of the same name
founded by Seleucus Nicator in memory of his father,
Antiochus. Admirably situated on a hill overlooking the plain
of Anthius, at the foot of the snow-covered hills known today
as the Sultan Dagh, it was already a great commercial center
when, sixty years before Saint Paul's arrival, Augustus made it
one of the six military colonies assigned to guard the high
plateaus. From its gardens one could see gleaming in the distance the blue waters of a large lake, one of several in the vicinity. The garrison was made up of Gallic soldiers from the
famous Skylark Legion. The ancient cult of the moon god,
Men, survived there in a Latin form. The Jewish colony,
greatly encouraged by the Seleucid kings, was flourishing and
many "God-fearing" pagans attended the synagogues (Acts
13:16, 44, 50; 14:1, 2, 5).

One Sabbath day Paul and Barnabas went to one of these
Jewish houses of prayer. Invited to address the congregation,
according to the custom, the Tarsiote complied. Speaking to
his Jewish compatriots, he skillfully argues three points; Israel
was the beneficiary and repository of God's promises. These
promises had been visibly fulfilled in Jesus, a descendant of
David, of the root of Jesse; therefore, Jesus, whom the people
of Jerusalem had rejected and slain, was the Messiah awaited
by the race of Abraham. The supreme proof was that He had
risen (Acts 13:1–41). To understand the amazement and joyful
surprise of these Hebrew exiles, far from their country, when
they heard such declarations, we must try to realize what the

expectation of the Messiah meant for a believer in those days, what feelings of love and hope filled his breast at the mere mention of this revered name. The missionaries were asked to speak again in the synagogues and the Jews and pious proselytes had long talks with them.

"The next Sabbath almost the whole city gathered to hear the word of the Lord. But on seeing the crowds the Jews were filled with jealousy." The community leaders, incensed at seeing these two newcomers winning more proselytes than themselves, set out to heckle them. The debate soon became stormy; Paul and Barnabas were unable to continue preaching. Then, angrily addressing those responsible for the maneuver, Paul exclaimed: "It was necessary that the word of God should be spoken to you first, but since you reject it and judge yourselves unworthy of eternal life, behold, we now turn to the Gentiles. For so the Lord has commanded us" (Acts 13:46). If the Apostle had needed another proof that his true destiny was to go, not to the Jews, but to the Gentiles, God had given it to him now.

For long months he remained in Pisidian Antioch, preaching successfully to the pagans. So successful was he that the Jewish leaders grew more irritable. Through the intermediary of some pagan women who were sympathetic to Yahweh, they brought influence to bear on the authorities without intervening themselves—a move which was not lacking in tact. Paul and Barnabas were persecuted and driven from the district. "They shook the dust from their feet," as the Master had counseled them to do on such occasions (Matt. 10:14; Mark 6:11; Luke 9:5; 10:11). And they resumed their journey.

Following the Roman highway, they tramped eastward, penetrating still deeper into the Anatolian peninsula. This province of Galatia, with rather indefinite frontiers, was bounded by Phrygia on the west, Cappadocia on the east, and Bithynia on the north; it was a transitional region between the high plateaus and the lower zone to the east. It was mainly a cattle-raising country, not very wealthy, though water still flowed through the splendid aqueducts which today exist only as desolate ruins, with a few fields of grain in the bottom lands. Side by side lived Lycaonian mountaineers, the Celtic-Galatian invaders, and many Greeks; the country was commonly known as "Gallo-Greece."

After four or five days on the march, Paul and Barnabas reached Iconium, the present day Koniah. After the sun-baked steppes, caked with salt deposits, it was a joy to the eyes, a veritable oasis. Paul undoubtedly thought of Damascus when he saw these fine orchards, irrigated by innumerable streams of running water. Only recently promoted to a Roman colony by the Emperor Claudius, Iconium was a great commercial center, a crossing point for roads leading to all parts of Asia Minor. The stay of Christ's missionaries in this city more or less duplicated their sojourn in Antioch: arrival at the synagogue, immediate success of their preaching with both the Israelites and the pagans, anger of the Sanhedrites, and machination against the missionaries. The city was soon divided into two factions, says the Book of Acts (14:1–5), some siding with the Jews, others with the Apostles. The mere presence of the two evangelists sufficed to raise the "sign of contradiction" which Christ crucified has always been in the eyes of men.

Was there a more specific, more dramatic reason for the opposition of the Israelite leaders at Iconium? A Greek apocryphal writing of the second century which enjoyed great success in the early Church, the Acts of Paul and Thecla—the same one from which we borrowed some features of the Apostle's portrait—relates a fascinating story in reference to this. In the house next to that where Paul was staying lived a pretty eighteen-year-old girl named Thecla. She was engaged to Thamyris, a young Greek. But through the open windows she heard the Apostle speaking, preaching so effectively that she was won over to his doctrine, especially to his teachings on chastity. Day and night she remained at her window, listening to his enchanting voice. Seeing this change in his fiancee, Thamyris became anxious and questioned her, only to hear the answer that she would not be his wife, that henceforth she belonged to Christ. Fury of the young man! Denunciation to the authorities! And suddenly Paul is thrown into prison. But then the gentle Thecla was transformed into a courageous virgin. She ran to the prison, won over the turnkey by giving him her finest bracelet, and entered the Apostle's cell and freed him! The story ends with a considerable number of prodigies, in which Thecla, for example, condemned to be burned, is miraculously preserved from the flames, which destroy the pagan bystanders—and many other even more astonishing episodes. This charming tale, which was retained in the Golden Legend, is unknown to the Book of Acts, which merely mentions that, forewarned of the intrigue against them, Paul and Barnabas took flight. They left behind them a church which was already well established.

Continuing eastward, they made their next stop at Lystra, located at the foot of the majestic extinct volcano of the KaraDagh. It was a little mountain town, a "Julian" colony as the inscription reads on the altar dedicated to Augustus, which was found there. The missionary's stay in this mountain village was to be as romantic as anyone could desire. It began pleasantly—almost too pleasantly! To begin with, Saint Paul performed a miracle there, one of the most startling miracles that can be attributed to him. Among those present when the Apostles first preached was a cripple, lame from birth, who had never been able to walk. As he sat listening to Paul, the latter fixed his glance upon him and realizing he had faith enough to be cured, said in a loud voice: "Stand upright on thy feet!" The man sprang up and began to walk (Acts 14:8–10).

The news of this miracle soon spread through the town and gave rise to a rather humorous incident. These good mountain folk were astounded at seeing such a prodigy taking place in their little town. Who could these two strangers be to possess such power? There was no doubt about it: one was tall, handsome, silent, Olympian—that was Zeus, the father of the gods; the other was thin, nervous, quick-moving, and a fine

speaker—Hermes, the messenger of the immortals! Had not
Zeus and Hermes visited this country before? Was it not told
that King Lycaon had received them at his table, but that having had the misfortune to offend them he had been changed
into a wolf? There were cheers for Zeus and Hermes, who had
returned to earth.

And now the good people came running to the temple,
bringing the priest, clad in white and with a garland of oak
leaves on his head, after him the temple servant bearing an
offering of salt and flour, and finally two fine white oxen
which they intended to sacrifice to the two divinities on the
spot. As the whole scene was played in the Lycaonian dialect,
Paul and Barnabas understood nothing at first. When they
finally realized that they were to be perched on the altar and
offered sacrifice, they protested and became indignant. Paul
spoke to the people, explaining that they were merely men
and telling them of the true God, which resulted in much dis-
appointment (Acts 14: 11–18).

Their sojourn at Lystra, which had begun so well, continued serene and fruitful. A Christian community was born in
which Paul found the one who was to be "his beloved son,"
and to whom he would entrust his spiritual testament—
Timothy, the son of a Jewish mother and a Greek father; he
was then still an adolescent but was already full of courage and
enthusiasm. However, the Apostle's enemies were watching
him. Lystra was only seventy-five miles from Iconium and
about ten day's journey from Antioch; and the watchful Jews
were not long in learning that the heretical missionary was
continuing in Lycaonium what he had done elsewhere. Their
emissaries arrived in Lystra, stirred up the people, and created
a riot in the course of which some of them dragged Paul outside of the town, stoned him, and left him for dead (Acts
14:19–20). The prophetic announcement that Christ had made
to Ananias, that He Himself would teach Saul what he was to
suffer for His name had been tragically confirmed. Beaten,
wounded, and breathless, the Apostle arose and was carried

back to the city by his disciples; was it at this time that those ineradicable wounds were inscribed in his flesh—those wounds in the feet, hands and side, whose symbol was to accompany his image throughout the centuries—the stigmata of the Crucified One, the seal of the Master, which are borne, whether visibly or invisibly, by all those who have given their lives to Christ?

The threat was serious, however. Realizing this, the Apostles departed the day after the incident and continued eastward. The little garrison town of Derbe was the point farthest east which they reached during this mission. The town was a simple fortress at an altitude of four thousand feet; since there was no commerce, the Jews were not established there and Christ's missionaries were able to preach the Gospel in complete tranquility. This was a marvelous exception for Paul; in this deserted plateau-country a church was born without conflict, without rioting, without outbreaks. At the end of a few months Paul was able to regard his mission in this place as completed.

Three long years had passed since the two companions in adventure had embarked at Seleucia. They felt the need of resuming contact with the Church at Antioch and of seeing once more the banks of the Orontes. Their direct route from Derbe would have been to continue following the Roman highway to the Cilician Gates and Tarsus. Paul chose another road and his choice reveals the energy and heroic resolution of this man of iron. At Lystra, Iconium, and Pisidian Antioch he had left Christian communities behind; now he returned to see them, in spite of the risk he might run into appearing there again. He reassured the neophytes, he exhorted them to persevere in the faith. Perhaps he explained to them his attitude with regard to the question of observances, that question which, as we have seen, was to trouble these Galatian churches. A priestly college was established in each city, and Paul, amid prayer and fasting, invested the new dignitaries by laying on hands. From Perge, where they also preached, the two Apostles reached Attalia, the little port where they had entered Asia Minor some thirty months before; they embarked on a mixed cargo ship carrying purple dyes and woolen stuffs. The Apostle of the Gentiles had completed his first missionary journey (Acts 14:21–26).

When Paul told his friends in Antioch of the results he had obtained, he could be justly proud that, once and for all, he had decided to find his glory in God alone and through the Cross of Christ. The Christian seed had been sown in Salamis, Paphos, and in other centers of Cyprus; five churches had been founded in Asia Minor, at strategic points from which they were to radiate throughout the peninsula. Hearing these accounts, the Christians on the banks of the Orontes were full of joy and admiration. Paul, Christ's pioneer, had indeed "opened to the Gentiles a door of faith" (Acts 14:26–27).

Discovery of Europe

Let us look forward two years: Saint Paul is in Troas, the small and illustrious province of the Homeric city, an advance point of Asia, opposite Europe and separated from it only by the straits of the Hellespont—the Dardenelles of our day, that swift-flowing river between two seas. Some months before, he had left on his second mission, having had his methods and his extensive program officially approved at the council of Jerusalem in the year 49. Had not the apostolic assembly decided that he would be entrusted with the task of preaching to the Gentiles, while Peter would occupy himself with evangelizing the circumcised? Heartened by this new assurance, he had said to Barnabas: "Let us return and visit the brethren in all the cities where we have preached the word of the Lord, to see how they are doing" (Acts 15:36).

However, the early days of this second evangelical expedition seem to have been marked by some strange sign, as if God wished to make His messenger understand that it would not be sufficient at this time to perfect his previous task, that his true destiny was always to push on. At the beginning of this second stage a rather unpleasant incident took place: Barnabas had wished to bring with him his cousin Mark, and Paul, who had not forgotten the young man's desertion on the previous mission, had objected; neither of the two apostles wished to yield, and they were forced to separate. Actually, like all the events in this Providential age, this one served the glory of Christ, for Barnabas left for Cyprus, to complete the evangelization of his countrymen. We may imagine, however, that this break with the one who had given him his first support, his master and his friend, must have been painful for a heart that knew the human value of friendship.

Of course, several candidates offered to replace Barnabas and Mark: Paul's personality was so radiant and his projects were so grandiose that volunteers were never lacking. Besides Titus, the faithful Greek who accompanied him to Jerusalem and who was to be, it seems, his companion throughout his life, he selected three aides, all of whom were to leave their mark on the history of Christian teaching. One was Silas, also called Sylvanus, one of those envoys—described as "prophets"—whom the apostolic assembly at Jerusalem sent to Antioch to announce its decrees (Acts 15:32); his title of Roman citizen was to be an asset for evangelical work while his friendship with Saint Paul, whose secretary he later became (1 Pet. 5:12), was to provide for valuable contacts. The second was Timothy, his son according to the spirit, that fine young man, of ardent faith, whom the Apostle had met at Lystra and won over to the Lord; his mother was Jewish, but because his father was Greek he had not been circumcised at birth, so Paul asked him to submit to this legal prescription in order to make it clear to all the Israelites that the decisions of Jerusalem were scrupulously respected (Acts 16:1-3). Finally, a third member had recently been added to the little group— the one to whom we are indebted for the account of all these incidents, Luke, the beloved physician. Apparently a Greek, he was cultured and intelligent and at the same time extremely sensitive. Beginning with the sojourn in Troas, the Book of Acts employs the first person in its narrative; this *we* (Acts 16:10) is proof enough that the faithful author was associated with the events described.

Thus, Paul had resumed the missionary's cloak and staff and traveled for months and months. He saw again the communities born of his labors; he notified them all of the decrees given by the apostolic council of Jerusalem. Everywhere he had the happiness of seeing that the Church of Christ was growing constantly and becoming stronger day by day. What, then, was the source of that sort of anguish he felt when, from the height of one of those hills which flock around Mount Ida, the legendary shepherd, he looked down on the coast of Europe, so near and so far away? Twice he clearly felt the Holy Spirit countering his plans. The first time, when he thought of descending to the coast of Asiatic Greece, to Smyrna or Ephesus; too soon! A second time, when he thought of reaching the interior, Mysia, Bithynia, Prusias, Nicea, and Nicomedia, the Spirit had ordered him, "Not that way!" What means did the Spirit use to indicate His commands to Paul? Perhaps he used Paul's illness as an instrument. Perhaps the thorn in the flesh became unusually painful. Would he not then have involuntarily prolonged his sojourn in Galatia?

He had obeyed, understood, and resumed his route to the West, and we find him now in Troas, the outermost gate to the Continent. This was the terminal point of the old world, which had been the scene of his first labors. Here the Apostle paused and reflected, on this same bank where Achilles died that Europe might conquer, where Alexander disembarked that Europe might leave its mark on Asia; here, a stone's throw from that new city, Alexandria of Troas, which Caesar had intended to make the capital of his States and which the emperors had enriched and showered with privileges in order to prove to the world the Trojan descent of the Julian race, so dear to Virgil. Out there, across the water, was the center of the Empire, and he knew, he felt, he surmised that nothing would be accomplished until Christ had penetrated Rome's Empire. But, on the other hand, he weighed the risks of such an undertaking; how would these men beyond the sea, who spoke such pure Greek and who boasted of being the only civilized people (they called the rest of the world "barbarians") receive a little Jew who spoke their language with a guttural accent and was quite incapable of quoting their poets with any skill?

But one night while Paul was painfully meditating, a vision illumined his thoughts: a man appeared to him, a Macedonian Greek, wearing the costume of his country, the chlamys, and the tall wide-brimmed headdress. He stretched out his arms and spoke, and what did he say? "Come over into Macedonia and help us!" Awakening, Paul arose. He had understood; the West was calling, full of nations who lived in darkness. Now he sensed that God Himself was sending him to preach His Word. A new act of the great adventure had begun (Acts 16:9–19).

Now the shores of Asia disappeared. Here was Samothrace, the isle sung by Homer, where Neptune took part in the battle of the sons of Priam. There was a stop for the night at the foot of the black cliffs beneath which, as the story ran, the Cabiri, (fire genies) worked incessantly at the forge of Hephaestus. The pagan mythology affected the traveler like a poisonous perfume. Did he take steps against it then? Not at all, it seems; he was in haste to reach the land which the Lord had pointed out to him. This mountainous, complex region was a rude, rugged land which the Greeks had long spoken of as a savage country, until that day when Philip and his genial son, Alexander, emerged from it to discipline them and to bring their glory to the world and to the ages. Since the Romans had taken possession of it, they had, according to their usual custom, laid out an excellent road, for strategic movements as well as for commerce—the Egnatian Way. This was the road that Paul was to follow.

Disembarking at Neapolis, the modern Cavalla, the Apostle did not pause there; this charming port, which is dominated from a steep hill by a replica of the Parthenon at Athens, was still too similar, with its mixed population, to the ports of Asia. It was three leagues from there, at Philippi, "the principal city" and a Roman colony—*Colonia, Augusta, Julia, Philippensis*, say the official texts—that Europe really began. Saint Paul was going to speak to the Philippians in the European style. He had undoubtedly heard that the sages of Greece liked to speak in the open air, beside the brooks dear to Plato; so it was in the open, "outside the gate, on the bank of the river," that he began to speak. His audience consisted mainly of women, and his success with them was rapid. It was known long ago how receptive a woman's heart can be to Christ's message of love; the Gospel proves this in many ways. A tradeswoman named Lydia, a seller of purple, was also conquered by the new doctrine; she had herself baptized there, in the running water of the river, with her whole family; and being a generous woman, she offered to receive the missionaries under her roof (Acts 16:13-15). The Apostle let himself be persuaded. His first contact with Europe was promising.

But had not Christ declared that He would always be a sign of contradiction? It would be out of keeping with the true destiny of his messengers for them to advance over roads carpeted with roses. Their first difficulties arose from a humorous incident. One day as the Apostles were returning to the river bank, they met a young female slave who was endowed with that spirit of divination which the Greeks called the spirit of Python, whence we have the term "*pythoness*"; Macedonia was swarming with them. This spirit could not have been too wicked, for the instant that the Apostles met the girl, she began to shout: "These men are servants of the most high God and they proclaim to you a way of salvation!" For several days following, she repeated her cries each time that she met them. Paul was obviously not at all pleased at being thus patronized by a pythoness in the presence of the pagans. Exasperated, he turned and cried to the spirit: "I order thee in the name of Jesus Christ to go out of her"; and the spirit immediately left.

The proprietors of the young slave, who had grown rich by exploiting her prophetic gifts, were furious at this turn of events. They threw themselves upon the missionaries, dragged them before the magistrates, and accused them of disturbing the peace and of teaching blasphemous doctrines—it is worth noting that, contrary to what had always taken place in the cities of Asia Minor, it was the pagans, not the Jews, who began the opposition in this case.

The crowd was riotous, shouting and storming. One could hardly hear the praetors ordering the culprits to be flogged; and in any case, if Paul and Silas had had the time to protest and to plead their privilege as Roman citizens, which in principle was supposed to spare them such ignominious punishment, their voices would have been lost in the hostile clamor. Beaten unmercifully and with their clothes in tatters, the missionaries found themselves in prison with their feet in stocks, and the jailer received orders to keep a close watch.

But in the middle of the night, while Paul and Silas were praying to the Lord, an earthquake took place, which was so violent that it shook the bars from the cell doors and the bonds from the two captives. Awakening with a start, the unhappy jailer thought they had escaped and was about to kill himself with his sword; Paul gently reassured him: "Do thyself no harm for we are all here." The man was so moved that he immediately repented, had his prisoners come out of their cells, asked to be instructed and baptized, and organized a little impromptu family party in his home, to celebrate his entry into the Church. Thus their stay at Philippi, which had taken such an unfavorable turn, ended on a happy note. Paul and Silas, finally recognized as Roman citizens, were released from their prison with apologies from the magistrates and left the city in high favor.

This colorful episode, which Saint Luke relates at length (Acts 16:11–40)—undoubtedly because he himself was to remain at Philippi for some time instead of accompanying Paul on the rest of his journey through Greece (the first person narrative ends at Acts 16:17)—is not merely picturesque. It shows that obstacles to Paul's apostolate could arise which were entirely different from those he had encountered in Asia Minor and which, while of a religious nature, were also sudden and violent.

At the next stops he was to meet the old opposition, the familiar hatred. Arriving in Thessalonica, the capital of Macedonia, a rich commercial city with a large Jewish colony, Paul and his companions preached first in the synagogue; after partial successes—and actually because of these—they soon aroused the anger of the Jewish leaders who, forming a mob of the city hoodlums, created riots, spreading disturbance throughout the city. A brave man named Jason, who had been so generous (and so imprudent) as to harbor the missionaries, was dragged before the "politarchs" and escaped from this predicament only with great difficulty. Paul had to take flight and make for Beroea, an agricultural town on a peaceful plateau. Things went better there. The Jews showed themselves more tolerant than those at Thessalonica, receiving Paul with respect, and studying the Scriptures with him for confirmation of his statements. Conversions were becoming numerous when a delegation of Thessalonian Jews arrived, fulminating against the missionaries. Again he had to flee in haste, abandon this perilous position and head for the coast (Acts 17:1–16).

Was it because the churches of Macedonia were created with such difficulty that Saint Paul always regarded them so affectionately? It was to them, to his beloved Philippians and Thessalonians, that he was to write some of his most beautiful pages. These Macedonian churches seem to have been rather defective in some respects. Did they owe to their barbarian ancestry those penchants for impurity and violence for which their spiritual father was to reproach them? And was it to their Greek elements that they owed a kind of skepticism toward the great mystery of the Resurrection? Ardent and faithful, excitable and docile, these first churches in Europe were typical of these primitive Christian foundations. Still encrusted with pagan mire, but full of love and enthusiasm—churches after Saint Paul's own heart!

Now it was the sea again. The ship rounded the triple point of Chalcidice and passed along the coast of Thessaly where, in the distance, fabulous Mount Pelion and Ossa were silhouetted against the blue autumn sky; entering the tortuous strait which separates the Euboea from the land, it passed the Euripus rapids when the tide was high. Standing on the bridge, the Apostle saw passing before him names which were illustrious for anyone raised in a Greek environment: Aulis, where Agamemnon assembled the thousand ships of the armada against Troy; Marathon, where a heroic Europe stayed the advance of Asia; the legendary mountains of Parnassus, Citheron, and Pentclicus, with the halo of the gods around them. At the point of Cape Sounion the temple of Poseidon, above the hyacinthine sea, challenged Christ's pilot. Finally, disembarking at Piraeus, he was able, by following the road which led directly to Athens, to observe at some length the marvel of marvels, that little tawny cage of gold and marble in which the Greeks claimed to have sheltered Wisdom: the Parthenon.

Athens, in the middle of the first century, was no longer the noble capital of Pericles and Phidias. It was a city in decline, still beautiful, but with that beauty which one finds in tourist views and in museums. It was full of idlers, brilliant and arrogant, constantly on the hunt for the latest news, exclusively concerned with being fashionable and well informed. Still an intellectual center, it included a large number of scholars and thousands of well-born adolescents who managed to combine a taste for learning with the pursuit of pleasure—those same youths whom Philostratus, in his life of Apollonius of Tyana, shows us on the beach at Phalerus, taking a sun bath in the mild autumn weather while they read, or practice rhetoric, or engage in endless arguments. The maddest ideas, the strangest theories, always find young minds to adopt and defend them. Oxford and Cambridge, or certain "advanced" intellectual circles in Paris, illustrate this atmosphere fairly well.

How did Christ's Apostle, the little Tarsiote Jew, react to this complex environment? What struck him most, what aroused him to indignation, was the quantity of idols at Athens. It must be admitted that there were a lot of them. The Acropolis was full of them, full to the point where there was not a foot of space to spare. They were all along the porticoed avenue that led from the Agora to the Dipylon. They were on the street corners, in the countryside, in the houses—practically everywhere. There was a flood of deifications; not only did Rome and Augustus have their temple, as might be expected—for the Athenian people were astute—but statues were erected to living men and women, and quasi-cults were built up around them, as in the case of the fair Berenice, whose moral life, moreover, was in no way exemplary. Paul, the pious Jew, for whom any physical representation of the divine was an abomination, was utterly outraged. The pagans themselves did not take this swarm of immortals too seriously: "Our country is so full of divinities," Petronius said smilingly, "that one is more likely to meet with a god there than a man." But Paul had no inclination to jest on such a subject.

It was on this point that he was to lead his attack. He did not dally among his compatriots; he had something better to do than to preach in the synagogue. He went to the Agora and spoke to anyone who chanced to pass. He met some philosophers there—the species was abundant—Epicureans and Stoics. Some curiosity developed concerning him: the new divinities announced by this little Jew had never been heard of before—one of them named Jesus and one called "Resurrection" (Anastasis). The intellectuals and professors smiled indulgently: "What is this babbler trying to tell us?" (They actually used a cruder slang expression, *spermologist,* which means exactly what it says.) Half curious, half ironical, they invited the missionaries to come and speak to them in public from the steps which had been cut into the rocky hillside of the Areopagus.

Then Paul made a mistake, the worst mistake of his career. He wanted to speak to these Athenian intellectuals in the kind of language they were accustomed to hearing. He believed he was being clever by beginning with a flattering allusion to the obviously religious spirit which was shown by this outcropping of idols, and that he would captivate them by astutely pretending that the "unknown God" to whom—in order to be sure they had forgotten none of the immortals—they had erected an altar, was Jesus Christ. Then he brought his argument around to the idea of one God, creator of all things, who brings order to the world, an idea which must have not been unpleasing to readers of Plato and Aristotle. On the whole, it was a very fine speech and is admirable when read from a Christian point of view; but it did not create any stirrings of faith and remained on an argumentative level. At this game a little Jew from Tarsus had no chance of overcoming the keen Athenian blades. When he came to affirming that God, in order to accredit Jesus, had raised Him from the dead, there was a great outburst of laughter. On this point, all the people of Athens, whether they were Stoics or Epicureans, were in agreement with old Aeschylus: "When the dust has drunk a man's blood there is no more resurrection for him." And they shouted to him: "We will hear thee again on this matter!" (Acts 17:17–32). It was an obvious defeat.

Occasional conversions took place, among them that of Dionysius the Areopagite, to whom so many mystical writings were later attributed. The speech was an error, therefore, from the viewpoint of immediate results, but one is tempted to call it a "happy mistake," to use an expression of Saint Paul himself.

The genius can draw from a defeat both a decisive lesson and the means of victory. In Athens, an intellectual city, Paul had just discovered that Christianity was not a philosophy and that it was not to be established by argument alone. He was never to forget this painful lesson. The following stop completed his understanding and appreciation of this lesson. The next halt was at Corinth, the great commercial center at the entrance of the Peloponnesus, "the city of the two seas," a city of which Horace had sung and which Pindar had called "happy Corinth, vestibule of the Sea Lord, joy of the young." The Greek city, razed by the Roman proconsul Memmius in 146 B.C., no longer existed in the time of Saint Paul, and only a few scattered vestiges remained: the fountain of Pyretus, the handsome temple of Apollo, whose six doric columns still stand intact amid the excavations on the "plain of death," the tomb of the celebrated prostitute Lais and that of the philosopher Diogenes the Cynic. A site that was so propitious for commerce could never remain unoccupied for long. While the convenient canal of today was not yet in existence, the merchants on either side of the isthmus had at their disposal a sort of track with rollers over which ships of small tonnage could be moved. The heavy cargo ships were unloaded on one side and reloaded on the other.

Thus the Romans had reconstructed a city, a Roman colony, and Julius Caesar had sent to populate it "a collection of misfit slaves," to use the expression of a contemporary. Comprising all the races, peoples, and colors of the Mediterranean, the population of Corinth was one of those picturesque but disreputable conglomerations such as one sees in the slums of Marseilles or Alexandria. From a certain point of view the reputation of the city was well-founded. The temple of Aphrodite Pandemos, which has been discovered on the Acrocorinthus, had a thousand prostitute priestesses; the other quarters of the city would have been well able to send reinforcements, for they were full of those loose women whom Paul unequivocally denounced. Since the time of Aristophanes, when a young girl was said to be *corinthizing* everyone knew what was meant, and in the jargon of the times, a *corinthiast* was what we call, in decent language, a procurer.

This was the atmosphere in which Paul proposed to teach the message of Him who said: "Be pure as I am pure!" But had He not also taught that "that which is lost" must be thought of first of all? Of course, on arriving in this whirlwind of paganism, easy love, and easy money, the Apostle at first showed himself somewhat reserved; he did not conceal this in his first letter to the Corinthians (1 Cor. 2:1–5). His recent experience at Athens had undoubtedly made him cautious. However, his first reception in the city was not unfavorable. A virtuous Jewish couple who happened to practice the same trade as himself, Aquila and his wife Priscilla, who had just been expelled from Rome because of the anti-Semitic measures of the Emperor Claudius, received him, gave him shelter, and accepted him as a partner. His two friends, Silas and Timothy, joined him and aided him in his preaching.

Paul was a little distrustful of the pagans, and it was in the synagogue that he again began to speak of Christ, but his results were worse than mediocre; contradiction and blasphemy were the sum of his harvest there. It is true that an important Jew by the name of Crispus had himself baptized, but his case remained exceptional and no one followed his example. When, at the same instant a "God-fearer," one of those pagans with monotheistic tendencies, showed himself friendly and sympathetic, the missionary realized his error. He had started off in the wrong direction, and he cried to the Jews: "Your blood be upon your own heads; I am innocent of it. Henceforth I will go to the Gentiles." And as if to support his preaching with the grace of the Holy Spirit, the Lord appeared to his disciple. "Do not fear," He said, "but speak and do not keep silence; because I am with thee and no one shall attack thee or injure thee."

Henceforth, Paul was to scatter the good seed by the armful. What mattered the color and odor of the earth on which it fell? It fell among the dock hands, the pimps, the sailors, the strumpets, and these humble, sullied souls probably received the word more readily than all the intellectuals of Athens. He remained in the great port city for a year and a half. Multitudes were to give themselves to Christ in this city of Aphrodite. It was in vain that the Jews in their fury went to lodge a complaint against Paul with Gallion, the proconsul; the latter, a wise and quiet man (he was the brother of the philosopher Seneca), and who seems to have been rather familiar with their tactics, sent them away dejected, and let Sosthenes, the head of the synagogue, work himself into a frenzy without taking notice. The Lord was obviously with His people.

Thus was born that church of Corinth to which Paul was later to write two of his finest letters. It is easy to imagine what he said to this church and what he was thinking while he was among her sons. Obviously he gave them moral counsels like those which, from Corinth itself he sent to the Thessalonians; the Corinthians must have needed them as urgently as the Christians of Macedonia. But he certainly told them something more, something that he himself had discovered in his dramatic personal experience. The result of this mission in Europe, and the conclusion he had reached, was that which he was later to summarize so admirably in his First Epistle to the Corinthians, namely, that if Christianity is not a philosophy, it is an undertaking involving one's whole being, an experience which resembles no other and a fully conscious risk.

"The world did not come to know God by 'wisdom,' it pleased God, by the foolishness of our preaching, to save those who believe. For the Jews asked for signs, and the Greeks look for 'wisdom'; but we, for our part, preach a crucified Christ— to the Jews indeed a stumbling-block and to the Gentiles foolishness, but to those who are called, both Jews and Greeks, Christ the power of God and the wisdom of God. For the foolishness of God is wiser than men, and the weakness of God is stronger than men" (1 Cor. 1:21–25). What the paradoxical success of Christianity in this evil city of Corinth had taught the Apostle was the real meaning of the power which had been driving him on for many years, that force which transcends all contradictions, redeems all weaknesses, that force which does not proceed from the intellect, but from faith and grace: the folly of the Cross.

CHAPTER 4

THE ROAD TO SACRIFICE

The Wide Open Door

There are, throughout the world, places whose very names exert a fascination on our minds: Egyptian Thebes, Delphi, Delos, Olympia or Ispahan, or Babylon. The mere mention of these syllables starts a flood streaming from the most sensitive zones of our consciousness, a mingled flood of images and memories. In antiquity, Ephesus was one of these glorious places. Illustrious for its wealth, famous for its beauty, regarded more or less as the rival of Athens for the science and culture of its citizens, it also bore a spiritual aureole as one of the great religious centers of paganism: a city like Naples and at the same time a Lourdes and a Chicago.

In our days the traveler who arrives there from the coast can hardly avoid being unpleasantly disillusioned. As soon as it leaves the fertile plain of Smyrna, the little puffing train crosses large marshy areas of willows, reeds, and daffodils from which flights of flamingoes and herons suddenly start up with shrill cries and flapping wings. Cut off from the sea by alluvial deposits, and abandoned to briars and fevers, Ephesus is not even one of those places notable for its ruins, where the archeological imagination can readily reconstruct the past, for the relatively ineffective excavations have not yet revealed its treasures. In a hollow marked by thickets of wild fig trees, blocks of marble, fragments of statuary, and a broken column emerge from a pool of stagnant water. It is the site of the temple of Artemis, which, we are assured, eclipsed the six other wonders of the ancient world. Few places on earth so strongly suggest the anguish which seizes one on seeing one of the cemeteries of civilization. Its appearance was certainly much different at the end of the year 53 when Saint Paul arrived there.

Ephesus, one of the eminent centers with Smyrna, Pergamum, Magnesia, and Sardis—the latter in decline—at that time presented the appearance of one of those Mediterranean cities where every circumstance seemed to attract money, luxury, and pleasure. The description which Saint John was to give, in chapter 18 of the *Apocalypse*, of "the great city, which was clothed in fine linen and purple and scarlet, and gilded in gold, and precious stone, and pearls," was probably suggested to him by the familiar spectacle of the port of Ephesus, "with cargoes of silver and gold, pearls and gems, rare woods and carved ivory, perfumes, spices, not to mention wine, oil, cereals, numerous cattle, and human merchandise—the slaves." On the slope of Mount Pion, with long avenues piercing its sprawling quarters, Ephesus proudly displayed groups of buildings which could compare with any in the known world: a theater with twenty-five thousand seats; a via sacra over a mile long; two agoras, one Greek, the other Roman and both surrounded by porticoes and colonnades; stadiums, gymnasiums; and, in the heart of the city, the gigantic hydraulic clock, famous throughout the entire empire.

But the finest and most illustrious of the monuments of Ephesus was the temple of the goddess Artemis—the goddess whom in Latin is named Diana—whose ruins now sleep beneath the black waters of a stagnant pond. The Artemis who was worshiped there was not the svelte, fleet-footed huntress of Greek fable, but a moon goddess who had come from the heart of Asia and who symbolized the all–fertile earth and the indomitable forces of life. She had long been venerated under the appearance of a more or less shapeless piece of stone which was said to have fallen from the sky. In the time of Christ it was the statue of a woman whose chest bore a score of breasts and whose legs appeared to be covered by a swarm of bees, the bees also being fruitful workers. An immense clergy served the temple; the high priest, the Megabyzos, had long sacrificed his virility to the virgin goddess; the priestesses were supposed to be chaste, at least during the time of their services. But many of the writers of the time, notably Strabo, have not concealed the fact that chastity was not in high esteem on the spring nights when the followers of Artemis went to plunge her statue into the sea in order to bring it into contact with the elemental forces. All through the month of Artemision (our April), pilgrim merchants came from all parts of Asia Minor to participate in the liturgical ceremonies and to have their future foretold, carrying on their business affairs at the same time. The threshold of Asia, starting point of caravan routes, a commercial center and a spiritual metropolis, Ephesus was indeed the wide open door of which Saint Paul was to speak to the Corinthians (1 Cor. 16:9).

It was from the interior that the Apostle reached Ephesus, coming from Galatia by way of Sardis and the valley of the Caystrus, the river which Homer said crossed "the meadow of Asia," and where, according to legend, the poet himself had been raised by the nymphs. This was in the course of his third mission. At the end of his second voyage, when he had embarked at Cenchrae, the port of Corinth on the Aegean, together with his dear friends Priscilla and Aquila, to return to Syria, his ship had made a short stop at Ephesus; it had been long enough for him to realize the importance this gateway of Asia might have in his plans of evangelization. He had refused to prolong his stay, but had promised to return (Acts 18:18–21).

After having passed some time in Antioch in the friendly atmosphere of that Christian community which had been associated with his days as a neophyte, the tireless messenger of the Holy Spirit had departed again. He was in haste to return to his Galatian children, with whom he had left part of his heart. He was in need of a new secretary; Silas had remained in Corinth, where he may have been working with Saint Peter, who was stopping in the city at that time; Timothy was directing the young communities of Achaia and Macedonia, passing from one Aegean port to another. For his traveling companion, Paul chose Titus, the young Greek convert whom he had brought to Jerusalem in the year 49 and who had occasioned the solution of the case of conscience concerning the circumcising of Gentiles (Gal. 2:1–3); henceforth, he was to be associated with all the apostles, and Paul unquestionably had a great affection for his "beloved son in the common faith" (Tit. 1:4).

Passing through Tarsus and, probably, through Derbe, Lystra, Iconium, and Pisidian Antioch, the Apostle had followed for the third time the central route through the Anatolian plateau. He had observed with delight that the seed sown in Galatia was bearing fruit a hundredfold, according to the promise. Then, crossing rugged Phrygia, he had descended to that shining coast from which the Holy Spirit had deterred him on his previous journey. It is more than likely that he had conceived and given a different character to this third stage of his apostolate. To bring the Gospel unceasingly to new peoples, as he had done previously, was good but it was no longer enough; an attempt at development and organization now appeared necessary. For this enterprise of supervising and instructing, which presupposed contacts with both the Asiatic and European communities, Ephesus was an admirable choice. He installed himself there.

Events at Ephesus had indicated that such an attempt was really indispensable. Paul may have been informed of the situation during his stop there the year before. In this young, primitive effervescent Christianity, there were little segregated groups which, quite unwittingly outside the church, were able to practice and believe according to norms which were not accepted by the average Christian. Thus at Ephesus, an Alexandrian Jew named Apollos, an eloquent man and learned in the Scriptures, had taught with fervor and correctly expounded everything concerned with Jesus. But he was familiar only with the baptism of John. That is to say, very likely, that taking up the teaching of the Baptist, he taught his disciples that holy water washed away sins if the soul agreed to do penance, but he did not teach Christian baptism, which is something quite different, a direct participation in the divine grace through Jesus, God made man, the victim immolated by the supreme pardon. Saint Paul's faithful friends, Priscilla and Aquila, who had preceded him to Ephesus, having seen the danger of this incomplete apostolate, had enlightened Apollos and then very tactfully had induced him to leave for Europe, where his combative energy had done wonders with the Jews of Corinth. On arriving in Ephesus, Paul was able to conquer this dozen or so of semi-Christians without too much trouble, and having laid his hands on them, he could see that the Holy Spirit had indeed descended on them, according to the promises of Pentecost, for they began to prophesy and to speak in tongues (Acts 18:24–28: 19:1–7). Trifling as the incident was, it nonetheless showed that it was not sufficient to sow broadcast the evangelical seed; it was also necessary to watch over the way it was growing.

Saint Paul was to remain at Ephesus for three years. This sojourn marks, in a certain sense, the culminating point of his apostolate, the stage of his full maturity. He was then in the prime of life, between forty-five and fifty years of age. His formative experiences were completed; he had become aware of the three great historical realities confronting primitive Christianity: Jewish tradition, Greek thought, and the Roman Empire. His personal authority was considerable; one gets the impression that he was surrounded by a full staff of assistants, Christians from practically everywhere; not only Titus and his beloved Timothy who joined him there, but Erastus and Gaius and Aristarchus, not to mention his faithful followers, Aquila and the devoted Priscilla. One thinks of a great missionary bishop, in the Congo or Gabun, aided and escorted by devoted young Fathers.

One may easily imagine what the Apostle's life was like during the Ephesian sojourn. At the beginning he had approached the city's influential Jewish colony and had spoken in the synagogue; the results proved disappointing, and he then did as he had at Corinth, breaking with his compatriots and turning to the pagans. In order to teach, he required a hall; he made arrangements with a professor by the name of Tyrannus to lend or to rent him his quarters when they were vacant, "from the fifth to the tenth hour," that is, from eleven in the morning to four in the afternoon, when the masters and students were dining and taking their siesta.

The Apostle's day was thus divided into two parts. Beginning early in the morning, he worked in the shop of his friend Aquila, and he worked hard if we may judge by the calluses on his hands, which he displayed so proudly. Then he went to the school of Tyrannus, where he spoke to his followers and to all those whom the evangelical message attracted, the great themes of redemptive love and fraternal charity and the promises of life and resurrection—those themes which we find superbly formulated in the great Epistles written in this period—were undoubtedly first expounded to his listeners in Ephesus. After the tenth hour, when the professor resumed possession of his quarters, where he taught grammar and philosophy, Paul continued his evangelical work in another way, by visiting those who had not been able to listen to him, the sick and the infirm. And in the evening, following the pleasant custom of this primitive church, all of the baptized gathered for the fraternal agape, in which the Eucharist was celebrated with bread and wine, as Christ had taught at the time of the Last Supper.

It was evident that the Holy Spirit was personally aiding this apostolate of Paul. In this primitive church, still quite close

to that day of Pentecost when tongues of fire had appeared
over the heads of the Apostles, there were frequent phenom-
ena in which the Third Person of the Most Holy Trinity manifested Himself: charisma, extraordinary graces, miracles, and
that mysterious "gift of tongues" which permitted inspired
persons to be understood by all their listeners, even if the listeners did not know their language. Saint Paul was to benefit
many times, during the years of his third mission, from direct
assistance of the Holy Spirit. "God worked more than the
usual miracles by the hand of Paul; so that even handkerchiefs
and aprons were carried from his body to the sick and the diseases left them and the evil spirits went out" (Acts 19:11–12).
The Apostle's command over demons became so well known
that Jewish exorcists attempted recourse to the same means. A
certain Sanhedrite named Sceva had seven sons engaged in
this curious practice. They pretended to drive out the devil,
crying: "I adjure you by the Jesus whom Paul teaches!" To
which the demon quite logically replied: "Jesus I acknowledge,
and Paul I know, but who are you?" And the possessed man,
on whom the Jewish exorcists had been testing this add formula, threw himself upon them and overpowered two of the
seven and maltreated them until they were forced to take
flight, naked and distressed. When the story got about in
Ephesus, it contributed greatly to Paul's glory. The incident
had an unexpected consequence. Magical practices were so
deeply rooted in their customs that they continued even
among the Christians; but Jews and Greeks, whether baptized
or not, learned their lesson from this event and brought to Paul
the books of magic and other occult sciences that they possessed; their value was reckoned at fifty thousand pieces of
silver. What a fine fire they made! (Acts 19:13–20).

  This unmistakable assistance of the Holy Spirit was anything but unwelcome, for one dearly gets the impression in
reading not only the Book of Acts but the Epistles written
from Ephesus by the Apostle, that this sojourn was disturbing
and frustrating. If we take literally a certain passage in the First

Epistle to the Corinthians (4:11-13), we must picture the missionary as overworked, penniless to the extent of knowing
hunger and thirst and lack of clothing, insulted often, and even
mistreated—considered by some, he says, as the scum of the
earth. This picture is by no means farfetched, and we can very
readily imagine this bold little Jew with the bandy-legs and the
guttural voice being chaffed, mocked, and heckled by many of
the people in Ephesus, where the best and the worst were to
be found together. Later, sending a message from Miletus to
his Ephesian friends, he was to allude to the tears and trials he
had borne in their city (Acts 20:18-21). The struggle against
stupidity, which is always, more or less, the lot of geniuses and
pioneers, was certainly the lot of Paul.

It was an incident of this kind which was to put an end to
the Apostle's stay in the great Asiatic port: Saint Luke, in the
Book of Acts, relates it with a verve which makes this perhaps
the most vivid page of this important and too-little-known
masterpiece. It was April of the year 56 and the feasts of
Artemis were about to begin. Great numbers of pagan pilgrims
had come to take part in the ceremonies of the nativity of the
goddess; the city was swarming with people. A certain
Demetrius, a silversmith by profession, who was dealing in
religious goods, selling statuettes of Artemis and little silver
models of her famous temple, spread out with his workers
through the squares of the city, vehemently denouncing Paul
and his followers. "Over the whole province of Asia this man
Paul has persuaded and turned away numbers of people, saying, 'gods made by human hands are not god at all.' And there
is danger, not only that this business of ours will be discredited,
but also that the temple of the great Diana will be regarded as
nothing, and even the magnificence of her whom all Asia and
the world worship will be on the decline!"

The agitator's colleagues all joined in and a riot soon broke
out. Bands of rioters ran through the streets shouting, "Great
is Diana of the Ephesians!" Commerce and religion combined
to harass the Christians. A delirious mob jammed the theater.

Two of Paul's helpers, Gaius and Aristarchus, were dragged off and were freed only with great difficulty. Paul was warned in time, probably by Aquila and Priscilla, who "risked their own necks" to save him (Rom. 16:3). He wanted to rush to the assistance of his friends; wisely he was prevented from doing so. A Jew named Alexander tried to make himself heard; was he a Christian, or was he trying to cry out that his compatriots had no concern over this devaluation of religious trinkets? At any rate he did not succeed in getting in a word. For two hours the uproar continued. It became so violent that the authorities finally grew anxious: what would the Romans say about all this? The town clerk appeared on the stage of the theater, obtained silence, and calmed the crowd, saying, quite reasonable, that if the silversmith's guild had anything to complain of, they had only to address themselves to the courts. Variable, as crowds always are, the agitated citizens of Ephesus agreed to disperse and return home (Acts 19:24–41).

But an affair like this must have weighed heavily on Paul's mind. There are moments in life when even the strongest feel weary. He was unwell physically; "the outer man was decaying" (2 Cor. 4:16). The work at Ephesus could be regarded as completed, or at least so well developed, that it would normally continue under its own impetus; instead of the dozen semi-Christians he had found on his arrival, there was now a strong and vigorous community. As for Paul, was he not "bound by the Spirit" to carry further the seed of the Good Tidings? Christian roots, radiating from Ephesus, had taken hold far from there, as far as the valley of Lycus, Colossae, Hierapolis, Laodicea (Col. 4:12–13; Acts 19:8–10). The immense world was awaiting its Apostle; indefatigable, Paul decided to resume his route and the baton of Christ's conqueror.

In fact the thought of all those people who were still awaiting the light and, even more so, of those whom he had already led to know it, had not left his mind all during the Ephesian sojourn. Among the heavy burdens which he had to bear, he had indicated, in his second letter to the Corinthians (2 Cor.

11:28), "the care of all the churches." If the expression "care of souls" ever had a strict meaning, it would be well applied to this great leader, who never abandoned a single one of his creations without remaining preoccupied with it thereafter.

One of the traits by which genius is recognized is the faculty of carrying on several enterprises simultaneously, of never letting oneself be so absorbed by the present instant as to neglect the achievements of yesterday or to ignore the future. At the same time that he dedicates himself to the task of the present moment, an Alexander or a Napoleon follows attentively the fate of what he has wrought in the past and never ceases to think of the future; on another level this also holds true for a Saint Paul. During his sojourn at Ephesus, when, as we have seen, his problems were numerous, it would have been excusable for him to devote himself to them exclusively, but this would have been the exact opposite of what he had planned to do: to strengthen the positions previously conquered by the Gospel.

The Ephesian years were marked, therefore, by the writing of letters addressed to his eldest daughters, the Christian communities born of him. At Corinth he had already composed some letters for the Macedonians. Do we know all of the Ephesian letters? Can we even readily date those which we still find in the New Testament? Thus, many of Saint Paul's com mentators attribute to this period of his life (while others date it from 49 to 50) the letter which he wrote to his beloved Galatians to correct a doctrinal deviation into which their churches were slipping, an error regarding the question of Jewish observances. It was probably at Ephesus that he composed the celebrated First Epistle to the Corinthians, which is one of his masterpieces. Disturbing rumors concerning the community at Corinth had come to his attention. Since he was unable to leave Asia, he had dispatched Timothy to the scene; then the messengers from Corinth had arrived, bringing better news (1 Cor. 14:17; 16:10–17). With a sovereign authority, the leader then wrote to his subjects in order to correct abuses and to set up principles of reform. "Stop arguing about the merits of Peter, Apollos, or myself! Watch out for your morality! And take care lest injustice pervert your community!" This was the substance of what he said to them. But—and this is another trait of genius—for him this event was an occasion for rising from a limited contingency to general truths; and this letter, written to prevent little Corinthian factions from quarreling and to deter a Christian from living with his father's wife, soared to the heights of morality and theology, formulating the doctrine of Christian marriage, defining the meaning of true charity, and affirming the resurrection of Christ with a power that is unsurpassed. It might well have ended with a hymn of triumph and of faith in the future.

So much for the past; but the future was of equal importance in the mind of our genius. What did the future hold for him? Paul had now permanently settled the question of Jewish fidelity; he had accomplished the maximum in the Hellenistic climate of Asia Minor and had even solved—fantastically—the problem of the relations of Christianity with Greek thought; he had tested his foundations and found them sound. But everywhere he went, in Philippi of Macedonia, at Corinth (in the person of the proconsul Gallion), even at Ephesus, where the mere shadow of the imperial eagle had sufficed to restore order at a time of disturbance—in all these places he had encountered the other great reality of the age, the weightiest reality—Rome. Henceforth, his mind was fixed on this powerful image. The name of the Eternal City now appeared in his discourses and writings.

Toward Pentecost of the year 56, at the hour when he was embarking for Macedonia, the last stage of his career had already been decided.

Clarion of the Spirit

The texts whose role in Paul's career we have just observed, these thirteen Epistles which the Church has retained as worthy of figuring in the Canon of Holy Scripture—a peerless distinction—must be considered with regard to the manner of their composition, their style, and their scope. The New Testament, taken as a whole, consists essentially of two biographies, those of Christ and Paul. We know the voice of Jesus only through the interpretation—inspired indeed, but human—of the evangelists; it is true that the tone of His voice is such that none would pretend to counterfeit it and that none of the other texts reveals "that kind of brilliance, at once gentle and terrible," which Renan described so well. In the case of the Tarsiote, on the other hand, we have the fortune of being able to read his life and thought, not only through the immediate witness of Saint Luke, but in pages in which he expresses himself directly.

Let us imagine Saint Paul as he composes one of these letters whose sublime phrases, coming to us across the centuries, pierce the heart like arrows when we hear a fragment of one in the course of Mass. It is evening; in the tentmaker's shop the looms have stopped, and the shuttle no longer draws the glistening thread across the woof. The flame of an oil lamp casts a circle of yellow light in which, hunched on his heels, a secretary holds the sheet of paper. Standing, now walking back and forth, now leaning against the frame of the loom, and leaping up at times when the inner fire seized him, the great Apostle dictated, dictated interminably, for hours on end.

All the letters of Saint Paul were undoubtedly composed in this way, not written, but dictated. This was the common practice of the ancients. The rich kept a slave in their homes as a secretary; the Apostle evidently had no slave, but one or another of his disciples gladly accepted the honor of this service; a Christian named Tertius, of whom we know no more than this, was the hand which held the pen for the Epistle to the Romans (16:22), and it is quite possible that for the First Epistle to the Thessalonians (1:1) this role was held in turn by the beloved Timothy and then Silas, or Sylvanus, who is later found as secretary to Saint Peter (1 Pet. 5:12).

It was no easy task to take dictation from such a genius! In the first place, the scribe's position was very uncomfortable; he was hunched on his heels, or, at best, sat with his legs crossed on a folded cushion, as the public scribes still do in Islamic countries. Besides, the writing material was by no means smooth; it was made of long bands of papyrus—the Egyptian reed whose name has served to designate our paper—bands glued together in two layers and showing many irregularities on the surface. The calami, notched reeds or goose quills, had an annoying tendency to scratch and make stains. When we examine certain papyri found in the Egyptian tombs and which are more or less contemporaneous with Saint Paul's letters, we get the impression that the scribe must have frequently drawn each character, almost in the Chinese manner. There is nothing surprising in the figures which a German scholar has established; for example, that in order to write the 7,101 words of the Epistle to the Romans, no less than fifty sheets and ninety-eight hours of dictation were required; if we consider that Saint Paul could devote to this task only his evenings, when all his other work was over, a letter must have required weeks, and that on the condition that it was not interrupted!

In general, before ending the letter, the author would add a few words in his own hand, as is sometimes done in our day at the end of a typewritten letter. On several occasions, at the end of one or another of his Epistles, Saint Paul has indicated that this was the case: "I, Paul, greet you with my own hand," he says to the Thessalonians, and he adds, "this is the mark in every letter. Thus I write" (2 Thess. 3:17). His writing must have been distinctive, in fact, if we may judge by the last paragraph of the Epistle to the Galatians, in which he says: "see with what large letters I am writing to you with my own hand!" Why large? In order to emphasize the difference, as we would underline a passage, or because his near-sightedness prevented him from writing a delicate hand, like a good scribe, or else because of his calloused hands . . . this simple and realistic detail is touching. When the letter was finished, if it was a short one, it was folded and sealed with wax; if this was not feasible, it was rolled up and slipped into a case. After which, nothing remained but to write the address, and also, frequently, the name of the bearer.

So much for the material composition, which was exactly the same as that of all correspondence of the time. This also holds true for the arrangement of the contents; it is that of all the letters which have come down to us from this period, whether the famous ones of Cicero, or that charming missive, recovered from the sands of Egypt, which a young soldier wrote home to his father from the base at Naples. Each letter comprised three parts: a sort of exordium, the *praescriptum*, containing the name of the writer and that of the addressee, together with friendly forms of greeting; then the body of the letter, developed more or less according to the subject; finally a conclusion which included farewells, good wishes, advice, and repeated greetings. All of Paul's Epistles are based on this outline. Were they personal letters or encyclicals of a sort, as we would say in our day, that is to say, texts addressed less to a specific individual than to a group, a community? The question has frequently been discussed, and there are numerous arguments pro and con. Some of these letters are unquestionably written to individuals, for example, the charming note to Philemon, the only one of the Apostle's texts which we may suppose he wrote entirely himself, in his own hand. Most of the Epistles have a quite different character; formally, there are some which are addressed to one man, as Titus or Timothy, or to a church pointed out by name, as the letter to Corinth or Thessalonica, for example; in effect, certain passages actually refer, as in ordinary letters, to concerns or personal affairs of the correspondents; but all of them, to a far greater extent, depart from these private matters, and rise to the level of general ideas, ideas of doctrine, of theology. It is thus extremely likely that, in dictating his letters, Saint Paul was actually thinking of a specific person or group with whose problems he was

familiar, but that he drew from these very problems the per-
manent and universal value which was to make his text useful
to many others.

The Epistles were therefore both authentic letters and
encyclicals of a kind. That it was the Apostle's intention to see
them distributed, copied, and communicated from community
to community, is more than likely: the preamble to the Epistle
to the Galatians and that of the Second to the Corinthians
leave no doubt of this. A letter of Saint Peter was to allude to
this transmission of the writings of Saint Paul in the primitive
Church, and there is nothing more stirring than some of the
records of the hearings in which Christians who were to die as
martyrs—those of Scilla, in Africa, for example—testified to the
venerations that they had for the Epistles of the great Tarsiote.
It is certain, then, that within the lifetime of the Apostle of the
Nations as well as in the tradition of the early Church, his texts
were recognized as bearing an eminent message, endowed
with an enlightening force, in short, as inspired. Why?

Was it Paul's literary qualities which established his fame as
a writer? Literary in just what sense? Was it his language? It is
certainly not a model for the student; even if we go back
beyond the Latin of the Vulgate, which in this part, not being
the work of Saint Jerome, is quite mediocre (and the majority
of modern translations are based on it); even if we refer to the
Greek, there is nothing to excite admiration. His language was
the common Greek used throughout the Near East, the Greek
of the *koine*, the Greek of the middle-class merchants rather
than the speech of the people—not too different, on the whole,
from that of Polybius or Epictetus. It was mingled with
Aramaisms and Hebraisms and with no small number of lively
popular expressions. Without being "incorrect," as Renan
described it, it was certainly not of exceptional quality.

Was his style any better? That depends. It is easy to criti-
cize it: excessively long sentences; uneven pace; dislocated,
choppy, and obstructive phrases; clauses awkwardly joined by
et and *car*; nested constructions, in which one thought suggests

another, which calls up a third, and so on, to the great defect
of logic. Yes, all these faults are to be found in Saint Paul. There
is something even more serious: a propensity to telescope the
thought, to suppress one of the essential details of the continu-
ity, to reason in terms of vague allusions and incomprehensible comparisons. When Bossuet said to him that he was
"ignorant of the art of speaking well," he was evidently thinking of all these points of criticism. And we can well understand
those who declare the Apostle of the Gentiles "obscure," even
taking into account the fact that this obscurity derives in large
measure from the historical and psychological conditions in
which the letters were written, conditions which too many
readers ignore.

But many experts have testified, too—and with excellent
arguments—that this Pauline style was of great value, that having "broken the narrow bounds and transcended that literary
atomism common to the men of his race," he was able, as
Father Grandmaison remarked, "to push forward an idea, to
rehandle it, develop shades of meaning, and give it a com-
pelling power that did not depend on the variety of figures of
speech and their juxtaposition . . ." This is true. "When the
presence of technical processes of the Stoic School is pointed
out to us in the Epistles, we may surely be permitted a discreet
doubt, but we cannot deny that something of the progressive
and harmonious character of Greek eloquence is reflected
here." Some enthusiasts have even placed certain passages in
Saint Paul close to the finest pages of Plato or of the famous
hymn of Cleanthes.

The fact that such opposite opinions can be sustained
proves that the essential merits of Paul the writer do not derive
from his language or his style, but from less formal virtues.
Certainly, he was neither a rabbi, nor a school philosopher, nor
a scrupulous furbisher of words and periods, but something
quite different, and it is precisely this difference that establishes
the great writer. Is the great writer he who possesses the gift of
striking formulas; who, by means of brilliant combinations of

terms, gives, as Mallarme says, "a new sense to the words of the tribe"? If this be true, what a writer was he whose most trivial page abounds with these inventions: "the good odor of Christ," "the man of sin," "the thorn in the flesh," "the folly of the Cross," and so many others! Profound, inexhaustible words, definitive formulas, which, after two thousand years and in spite of the blunting effect of translations, still shine with such brilliance.

Again, is a great writer the one who knows how to introduce into a development such a wealth of material and in such concentrated form that one can neither add, nor change, nor omit an iota without damaging the essence? If this is the case, what a writer he was! There is not a single one of his Epistles that does not contain one of these compact gems, these perfections. Let us listen to him, in the First Epistle to the Corinthians, crying out to mankind the promise of the Resurrection.

"Behold, I tell you a mystery: we shall not all sleep, but we shall all be changed—in a moment, in the twinkling of an eye, at the last trumpet. For the trumpet shall sound, and the dead shall rise incorruptible and we shall be changed. For this corruptible body must put on incorruption, and this mortal body must put on immortality. But when this mortal body puts on immortality then shall come to pass the word that is written, 'Death is swallowed up in victory! Oh Death, where is thy victory? Oh Death, where is thy sting?'" (1 Cor. 15:51–55).

Such a passage, justly famous, is characteristic of the Apostle's style, of his evocative power, of his inner violence, of his skill in using metaphor and in drawing from abstract ideas images which capture the imagination. But there are other passages, written in an entirely different style which are not in the least inferior. Among these is one taken from the same Epistle, and no less famous, in which he defines in minute detail the characteristics of the love of godly men: "charity is patient, is kind: charity does not envy, is not pretentious, is not puffed up, is not ambitious, is not self-seeking, is not provoked: thinks no evil, does not rejoice over wickedness, but rejoices with the truth; bears with all things, believes all things, hopes all things, endures all things" (1 Cor. 13:4–7). What a penetrating analysis—and in a half-dozen lines! How many truths in these few words!

But beyond his gift of phrase-making, his skill in development, and even the range of his style, the extent of which is indicated in the two passages we have just re-read, what makes Saint Paul the great writer that he is, is that ever-conspicuous inner violence, that force which gives an invincible drive to his uneven sentences, his occasionally ponderous developments and unintelligible figures of speech, and imposes all this on the reader's mind as a single irresistible reality. Such art as this is beyond the professors and texts books; but it is art, great art, and all the greater in that it is unconscious and spontaneous. His purpose is never writing for the sake of writing; still less does he aim at a masterpiece. He throws out his phrases as a fountain spouts water, or rather as the volcano jets forth its lava, like a surging flame.

And it is this—this passion, this violence, this surge— which assures the integrity of this literary personality—that is so rich and so complex. There is much of the orator in this writer; a penchant for the rhetorical, a cadenced rhythm which is often perceptible, a sort of swing which derives from the oral style of the Semites and the Orient. There is something of the poet in him, which at certain moments—and especially when he speaks of the great divine drama of which Christ is the center, the drama of salvation—soars off in lofty flight, like a great bird above vertiginous depths. There is in him also a little of the rabbi, of the former student of Gamaliel, who is not ignorant of Scriptural argument, nor of the art of using quotations. There is something of the dialectician in him, a skill worthy of the subtlest Greeks, which enters spontaneously and almost unconsciously into the development of the "diatribe," so dear to the popular orators of Athens and Corinth, Cynics or Stoics; what a distinctive way he has of personifying an adversary, of representing him as flesh and blood, of overwhelming him with questions and answers at the same time, and of throwing words at him with machine-like rapidity!

Finally, there is something of the philosopher in him, not in the present-day sense of the word perhaps, nor in the classical sense, but in the sense in which one may use it of a man so magnificently gifted for intuition and deduction, for the most lucid analysis and the most arduous syntheses. Yes, there is all this in Saint Paul—and much more besides! He is ironic and tender, thoughtful and impulsive, now violent and again persuasive—he is all of these things together, and these disparate gifts, instead of offsetting each other and ending in discord, are united in so powerful a reality that, unfamiliar as it may be, one recognizes his "style" at first glance. But what is the force that unites and harmonizes these opposing elements? Nothing else than the élan vital itself, the vital drive of a personality and existence which have few peers in history.

This is the definitive explanation: if Saint Paul is a great writer, it is because he is not a writer first of all, but a man. We know that each of his texts was bound up in its development with events and people; they are not the products of a mind securely sheltered in the refuge of a library, but the works of a conqueror, of a fighter, whose whole life was risk. His purpose, thus, was not to expound a doctrine, but to inform, reform, and affirm. All he thinks and writes, he thinks and writes in full flight, swept on by the violence of the struggle itself. And this spontaneous attitude of his is the same required of all who practice Christianity, for the Gospel is not a system of thought but a story, a drama; and what matters most is not to demonstrate it but to live it.

Thus, Saint Paul's personality was spontaneously incorporated in the message which was given him to bear, and as this personality was marvelously rich, varied, and complex, and as he also had realized the rare achievement of inner unity, it is his personality which, when all is said and done, smoothes out all imperfections in his literary work and makes it what it is, a block of marble or of steel.

But is this the only explanation, the ultimate explanation? Certainly not. In a picturesque and stirring passage, Saint John Chrysostom, the most pertinent perhaps of the early Fathers up to the time of Saint Augustine, has recalled the emotion he experienced when he read the Epistles of Saint Paul: "I recognize the voice of a friend; I have almost the impression of seeing him and hearing him in person." And he adds: "Then I exult joyously and arise from my sleep; the sound of that trum pet of the Spirit exalts me and overwhelms me with happiness." These last words tell all there is to tell.

If Saint Paul is the great writer whom we see, it is not merely because of his forceful personality, the subtlety of his intellect, the power of his genius; rather it is because he was the "trumpet of the Spirit." He who said of himself that he was "set apart from his mother's womb," who on the road to Damascus, was called by name by Christ Himself, had within him a far more effective force than any talent or genius, and this force was nothing else than that of God. "Walking according to the Spirit, living according to the Spirit," he also spoke and wrote according to the Spirit. As we have seen, we condemn ourselves to understanding nothing of his character if, in seeking to explain him, we pass over his immediate relations with God. Likewise, we shall be totally deceived as to the meaning and scope of his texts, if we fail to see there, above all, the ineffable seal. Far more than a writer, a dialectician, or theologian, Saint Paul is an inspired genius, and in the fullest and most exact sense of the term, since he is at once a genius and a saint. His art is merely the expression, pouring from his lips, of the overwhelming presence which dwells within him.

Can we doubt that he himself was not aware of this, who one day gave vent to this anguished query: "Is it truly I who am capable of all these things?" Whether we are concerned with the vicissitudes of his life or the arcane of his works, we must never for an instant lose sight of the fact that this adventurer in thought and action was above all an adventurer according to the Spirit.

The Road Which Leads to Calvary

Once more the Holy Spirit was needed to guide the steps of His witness and to give strength to his soul. For when he left Ephesus in the year 47, after the silversmith's riot, Paul was prey to an extreme despondency. In the eyes of his enemy, had he not appeared as a coward in abandoning a post which had become too dangerous? What was to become of that church which he had founded at the cost of such efforts? And his beloved community at Corinth, which had given him so much anxiety—had it found again the peace of Christ since he had written to the Corinthians? All this was a source of anguish.

Moreover, the journey he was beginning from Ephesus was to impress him quite differently from the preceding ones. He was no longer visibly submissive to a carefully thought out plan, a purpose logically pursued, but above all appeared to be obeying the actions and reactions of events and emotions. Paul was aware of this himself but he trusted as always in the One who, once and for all, had taken his life in hand. On several occasions during this period, he was to repeat that he was "bound by the Spirit" or "led by the Spirit from city to city." For the Spirit knew the ultimate explanation, the end toward which this almost erratic course was leading, which was nothing more nor less than sacrifice. And deep in his heart, Paul, too, undoubtedly knew this.

Before taking the road for Jerusalem, where he was to discharge a mission to the first of all the Churches, the Apostle desired to see once more his daughters of Troas, Macedonia, and Achaia. Accompanied by Timothy, therefore, he set out again for the north and stopped anew at Troy, which was a busy center of traffic, a junction between Macedonia and Asia Minor. He had intended to meet Titus there, whom he sent to

Corinth several months before to see that the precepts in his letter were being followed. But the disciple was not at Troy. Paul could not stay, and set out to meet him. Reaching Macedonia was difficult: "Our flesh had no rest; we had troubles on every side, conflicts without and anxieties within." Finally Titus arrived, bringing better news: things had improved at Corinth, so it seemed (2 Cor. 7:6–7).

Comforted by the report of Titus, Paul then began to write his Second Epistle to the Corinthians. Thus the beginning of the letter is full of joy and confidence, and affection. "The God of all comfort, who comforts us in all our afflictions" had consoled Paul; the trial which God had made him undergo with regard to the Corinthian Church now took on its full meaning, as disappointments and difficulties showed the value of true love. From now on Paul, the founder, the father of this community, was happy; he gloried in his children.

Suddenly—as anyone reading the Epistles will note—the tone changes. Mildness and gentleness are succeeded by threats and indignation. It is not the tenderhearted man who is speaking now; it is the leader, the fighter. What has taken place? Had new messages arrived from Corinth, or had more intensive conversations with Titus led Paul to discern certain difficulties? Evidently, opposition had developed against him and his influence; some intruders of uncertain origin and directed by persons unknown, had fomented a cabal against him. They accused him of being lukewarm and irresolute, and at the same time violent and authoritarian; they ridiculed his incomprehensible letters, his dubious eloquence; a madman, an imposter—that is how they pictured him! And now he was going to defend himself! And what a defense! A series of dazzling, moving phrases which reflect his complete dedication. This message was much more than a personal plea.

Speaking to these people who criticized him so unjustly, he succeeded in telling what he had never spoken of to anyone: the extraordinary graces with which the Lord had endowed him, the secrets of his mystical life. An overwhelming testimony!

The man who dictated these pages was obviously distressed, wounded in heart, but he knew, felt, and proclaimed that his sorrows themselves had a meaning, that his anguish served the cause to which he had consecrated his life. And it was then that that sublime formula leaped to his lips: "when I am weak, then I am strong!"

This letter, carried by Titus, probably reached Corinth shortly before Paul himself disembarked there. He wanted to study the situation firsthand. There was another reason which led him to visit the Christian community in one of the richest cities of his time: at the apostolic assembly in Jerusalem in the year 49–50, he had formally promised that the communities founded by him among the Gentiles would not forget the Mother Church, born in the vicinity of the temple and which, being made up of people of little social standing, had always suffered from a poverty bordering on misery. This work of charity in action, the alms for Jerusalem, was dear to the Apostle's heart. He rightly saw in it a means of expressing concretely the unity of the church, a unity above all differences of fortune, class, race, and observances. In the communities of Galatia and Macedonia, he had already earnestly recommended this work of mercy; he had spoken of it, too, to the Corinthians in his first letter, and chapters eight and nine of the second letter were devoted entirely to persuading them— with equal skill and delicacy—to show themselves generous. It seemed to him that it was not enough to write; he went there in person.

He found the Corinthian community had quieted down. He remained there all through the winter of 57–58, applying himself to restoring order where this was necessary and to consolidating his work. Calm returned to his heart. But this man of fire was so made that he could really live only when he was looking to the future. He had bound himself to the two realities of the present; he could see, too, that at Jerusalem he would meet with other obstacles; but beyond all this, what he saw was Christianity taking a new step forward, the Gospel conquering Rome itself, the center of that Empire of which he had as yet known only the outermost parts. As he watched the ships setting sail for Italy on the calm waters of the long Corinthian gulf, Paul felt his thoughts fleeing with them toward the city whose image already obsessed him.

And so it happened that, during this sojourn at Corinth, he wrote his famous Epistle to the Romans, unquestionably his masterpiece and the keystone of his theology. He knew that an important Christian community already existed in the capital. In order to announce his visit, and also, no doubt, to forestall the machination of adversaries, he decided to make a full presentation of his thought and doctrine. What did Christianity mean to him? That is what he wanted to make them understand. Christianity is the religion which saves men, all men, and which alone can save them. The pagan religions were mere lures, which, far from raising man above himself, debased and degraded him. And the Jews themselves were no better; though heirs of the Promise, they had resisted the Holy Spirit! No, the only salvation was in the Gospel, the message of justice and love. And what the great theologian now expounded was the whole plan of the Redemption, that plan according to which God, Christ, and man were united, through which sin and death were swallowed up in the victory of the Resurrected, through which eternal life was the supreme accomplishment of those who were saved in Christ and by Him. Full of hope, heavy in doctrine, the pages of the Epistle to the Romans must have required night after night of dictation before the hefty sheets were filled up; the whole winter of 57–58 was devoted to this.

Meanwhile, the collection had been continued by Paul's collaborators, whose numbers had again increased; the leader's staff was now complete. There were the faithful Titus and Timothy and the beloved physician Luke, whom they had met in Macedonia, Sopatros, Secundus, Aristarchus, Gaius, Tychichus, and Trophemus—men from all the communities, and all of them fervent. When the work at Corinth was finished they decided to leave for Jerusalem. But it was ordained that their difficulties should continue. At the instant of embarking, Paul was informed of a serious danger: some orthodox Jews, faithful to the Torah, were plotting to rid themselves of him. In the hubbub of a great port, in the midst of sailors, stevedores, travelers, a stabbing would have been a simple matter. They were therefore forced to take the land route, the long route through Macedonia, whose flagstones had already been trodden by the sandals of the Apostle several times. In order not to awaken suspicion, his companions were sent on ahead; they would wait at Troy (Acts 20:5–6).

What was the Apostle's state of mind at this time? Was he not weary of seeing obstacles incessantly rising before him? It was more than a year since he had left Ephesus and in that time he had been spared no respite from troubles and anxieties. But he was watched over by the Spirit, who always advances directly, though by devious paths. At Troy he gave proof that He had not abandoned His witness. One evening, making the most of his short stay in that city, Paul was speaking to a gathering of the faithful. They were about to celebrate the liturgical repast. There were many lamps in the third floor rooms where the meeting was held; it was warm and they had left the window open; a young man named Eutychus, who was sitting on the sill, grew drowsy and fell off. Everyone rushed down the stairway, Paul with the others, but the boy was dead. "Do not be alarmed," said the Apostle, "life is still in him!" He went up into the room, broke bread and ate; would He who had instituted the Holy Eucharist and promised life through His flesh and blood let death conquer in this instant? When Paul left the house at dawn, his act of faith had found its reward. God had wrought the miracle: Eutychus was alive (Acts 20:7–12). Paul knew this: the Lord had never abandoned him.

From now on Paul appeared to be driven by a fever; he was in a hurry to arrive in Jerusalem. Was it merely to hand over to the brethren the alms he had collected? Or was it for another reason, known only to his most secret soul, that soul which received the light of God? At the conclusion of his stay in Troy—it had lasted a week—the Apostle set out again. He sent his companions ahead by sea to Assos; he went on foot, probably so he could see again on his way some of the small groups of Christians. He did not wait in this ancient port, where monuments of Homeric times still existed—the massive Acropolis, the Cyclopean ramparts; a ship was leaving for Tyre and he embarked on it. Heading straight south, they saw passing to starboard the joy and beauty of the islands: Lesbos and its rosy villas; rugged Chios, with its fiery wine; and wealthy Samos, like a platen leaf floating on the water. At last the ship touched at Miletus, a second-class port where it seemed rather surprising to make a stop.

However, Paul stayed there. He did not wish to return to Ephesus, his beloved Ephesus, though it was not far and was even closer in his heart. The impatience of the Spirit was driving him forward; to return to Ephesus would be to return to the past, to retrace his steps. Jerusalem! Jerusalem! He wished to be there for the days of Pentecost, the feast of the Holy Spirit. However, as he set sail again, his heart contracted with emotion. He could not pass so close to his Ephesian friends without giving them some sign. A messenger went ahead to notify them. They ran to meet him and there on the shore, a few feet away from the ship that was to bear him toward his destiny, Paul spoke to them.

This improvised allocution on the beach of Miletus is perhaps the most poignant page that we know of by the Apostle. As in the case of the great prophets, the future was present before him. And what a future! Perhaps he would never again on this earth see his friends, those friends dear to his heart; the counsels which he gave them sounded like sentences from a testament.

"And now behold, I am going to Jerusalem, compelled by the Spirit, not knowing what will happen to me there; except that in every city the Holy Spirit warns me, saying that imprisonment and persecution are awaiting me. But I fear none of these, nor do I count my life more precious than myself, if only I may accomplish my course and the ministry that I have received from the Lord Jesus, to bear witness to the Gospel of the grace of God. And now, behold, I know that you all among whom I went about preaching the kingdom of God, will see my face no longer . . . . Watch, therefore, and remember that for three years night and day I did not cease with tears to admonish every one of you. And now I commend you to God and to the word of His grace, who is able to build up and to give the inheritance among all the sanctified . . . . Remember the word of the Lord Jesus, that He Himself said 'It is more blessed to give than to receive'" (Acts 20:22–35).

At these last words, he fell upon his knees and prayed aloud. All those present joined in his prayer. A great emotion seized their hearts. Many let their tears flow freely. Then the sailors, to the rhythm of a chantey, pushed off from the shore. And for a long, long time, until the yellow sail had disappeared over the horizon of the islands, the Ephesians remained on the shore, disconsolate.

And now it was the sea again. In three days, sailing via Chios, the island of the black wines, and Rhodes, the isle of roses, Paul reached Patara, on the coast of Lycia, one of the famous sanctuaries of Apollo. There he changed ships, having chanced to find a vessel which was sailing directly to Phoenicia. Cyprus was on his left, behind him. Cyprus and the memories associated with it: his first mission, Barnabas, the proconsul Sergius Paulus—how many events had taken place in the fifteen years which had elapsed since then! And after a crossing of four or five days, Tyre and its cliffs appeared.

Tyre is no longer the showy metropolis of the Phoenician splendors sung by the Bible, but it is still a lively little port stocking and selling "Tyrian purple" shellfish. And here again, the Holy Spirit manifested Himself. This time it was to the faithful of Tyre that He revealed the future, the dangerous future which was lying in fate for the missionary.

They begged him not to leave, not to go to Jerusalem, to remain among them. But no, it was impossible; one does not resist the Spirit's orders. And while they stood gathered on the bank and prayed together as with a single heart, Paul climbed aboard his ship (Acts 21:1–6).

His voyage was now approaching its end. Disembarking at Ptolemais—our Saint Jean D'Acre—Paul and his companions stopped just one day in order to greet the little Christian community there; then, following the highway which circles Mount Carmel, they reached Caesarea in one day's journey (Acts 21:7). The town, which was both an administrative center and a garrison, included a strong nucleus of Christians. The leader of the community was Philip, one of the seven deacons, the same whom we saw earlier baptizing by the roadside the officer of the queen of Ethiopia, the eunuch with the heart full of good will. After having evangelized southern Judea and Samaria, Philip had established himself at Caesarea with four of his daughters, who exercised in the Church the rather vague role of prophetesses (Acts 21:8–9; cf. 8:5–40). Thanks to his rapid crossing, Paul had a little time to spare, for he had no desire to arrive in Jerusalem before Pentecost; he therefore accepted the deacon's invitation and spent several days in his home.

It was at this time that, in a third intimation, the Holy Spirit spoke: once He had spoken directly to Paul's soul, once to the Tyrian community; now he employed another means. A prophet arrived from the mountains of Judea, one of those seers who were so numerous in the early church, a man named Agabus; he wished to see Paul. The Apostle was already acquainted with him and knew that his power was authentic, for it was he who, at Antioch in the year 44, had predicted famine, which led Paul and Barnabas to bring aid to the brethren of Jerusalem (Acts 11:27–28). The instant he came into Paul's presence, the seer took Paul's cincture, bound his own hands and feet with it and exclaimed: "thus says the Holy Spirit: the man whose girdle this is, the Jews will bind like this at Jerusalem and they will deliver him into the hands of the Gentiles!" It was a symbolic gesture, in the tradition of the ancient prophets of Israel; thus Jeremiah, to predict to his compatriots the Chaldean captivity, had saddled himself like a donkey and paraded through the streets; thus Isaiah went about naked to show in what condition God would leave His people in the day of His wrath.

In the face of such an obvious warning, what was to be done? Together, Paul's companions and the Christians of Caesarea sought to deter him; weeping, they begged him not to go up to Jerusalem, but the hero, terribly calm, answered (and what a shudder of anguish we sense in these words!): "What do you mean by weeping and breaking my heart? For I am ready not only to be bound but even to die at Jerusalem for the name of the Lord Jesus." Failing to convince him, the disciples acquiesced. "The Lord's will be done," they murmured (Acts 21:8–14). There are situations in which these are the only appropriate words.

Now he was to take the road to Jerusalem, the road to the very place where Christ died for the salvation of men. Had not Paul himself written that he should complete in his flesh what was lacking in the Passion of Jesus? And had he not said that the very core of Christianity was the mystery of the Cross, the redemption by the Blood? The One who had been guiding him for many years now wished him to assume his own share of that Passion and that sacrifice. It was fitting. It was necessary. And as always, Paul obeyed the order of the Holy Spirit.

CHAPTER 5

THROUGH BLOOD TO ROME

"Thou has borne witness to me in Jerusalem" (Acts 23:11).

To go from Caesarea, on the coast, to Jerusalem, must have taken at least three days. Having crossed the rich plain of Sharon, where the wheat was already golden, Paul went up from Lydda and followed the rolling hills of Judea for hours before catching sight of the holy gates toward which the psalms of the pilgrims sighed. Many friends and disciples had accompanied him; Pentecost was a great feast in Israel, at which great numbers of the faithful assembled in front of the temple to thank the Lord for having given Moses the revelation of the Law. As the witness of another, more definitive revelation, what did the Apostle of the Nations think and feel on returning to the city of the Chosen People?

We may be sure that he was not without some anxiety. Everywhere he had gone, for many years, and indeed even quite recently at Caesarea, Tyre, Miletus, and elsewhere—he had felt at home among Christians of universalist tendencies, for whom there was "neither Greek, nor Jew, nor circumcised, nor uncircumcised." Such men were akin to his spirit and to his blood; such were the communities of Asia, Macedonia, and Greece, which had gladly heard the veritable message of the Lord. But Paul was not unaware that the Holy City was still dominated by the other tendency, that of the Christians who had remained attached to the letter of Jewish observances and who had accepted half-heartedly the decisions of the "Council" of the year 49–50. He had found the Judaizers opposing him and his work at Antioch, as he had in Galatia and Corinth; what reception would they offer him at Jerusalem?

He knew, of course, that James was still there, and still completely loyal; James, the elder of the Church, who seven years before had swung the balance in favor of the Pauline thesis. But, besides him, on whom could the Apostle of the Nations count? Peter was far away—at Rome, so they said. Far away, too, was Barnabas, and Silas, and all those whose authority might have backed up his own. If a shift of opinion had returned the leaders of the Christian community to their former position, Paul's apostolate would be threatened, and his entire work challenged. In any case, there would be a new battle to fight. It was a scene familiar to men of genius, to all those who accomplish great things; they advance so rapidly that their former friends are first astonished, then annoyed, and end by regarding them with distrust. It was this painful hiatus which quite understandably disturbed Paul as he entered Jerusalem on the feast of Pentecost.

As a matter of fact, the conflict he feared did not develop. Having arrived in the Holy City, where a good-hearted Cypriote named Mnason, a Christian of long standing, had offered him food and lodging, Paul presented himself to the members of the Christian community. He was received with open arms. The very next day a meeting was held at the house of James, participated in by all the Elders of the Church, together with the Apostle of the Nations surrounded by his friends. There was an exchange of peaceful greetings, and then Paul spoke. "He related in detail what God had done among the Gentiles through his ministry" (Acts 21:17–19). Without doubt, he did not fail to recall that, in all his activity, he had remained strictly faithful to the decisions of the assembly; nor did he fail to stress, as evidence of his devotion to the Mother Church, the results of his collection among the other communities. His argument was successful; all present congratulated him, praising God for having wrought such great things through him.

However, a supplementary precaution appeared indispensable. In the Judaizing circles of the capital, many excellent Christians were suspicious of the Apostle's boldness. Was it not said that, through his teaching, he had led all the Jews who had settled among the pagans to break with the Law of Moses, that he had dissuaded them from having their children circumcised and from respecting the holy observances? It was necessary to put a speedy end to such rumors, especially since the arrival of the great missionary in Jerusalem had created a sensation. It was agreed that it would be best for Paul to perform some act in public, which would testify to his attachment to the Mosaic law. Anyone else would have refused to comply with such a demand; did not his entire life and all his writings answer for his fidelity to Israel? But "charity is humble," accepting and bearing all things; he accepted.

As it happened, an excellent occasion presented itself for the desired gesture. Four Christian Jews, following the ancient usage, had made a vow to consecrate themselves to the Lord, pledging that they would abstain from wine, and sexual intercourse and that they would not cut their hair. They called the people who bound themselves by such vows *nazirs*; some took the vows for their lifetime this had been the case, in Biblical times, of Samson, and undoubtedly, quite recently of John the Baptist— others bound themselves only for a time, ordinarily for a month, and in this case, on completing their devotional retreat, they were supposed to offer a sacrifice which the Book of Numbers determined as follows: a lamb of one year, a ewe of the same age, unleavened bread, cakes, and a ram. The formality was obviously expensive. The four Christians had taken the vow for thirty days, but being paupers, were unable to satisfy the requirements for the sacrifices. Therefore, the elders advised Paul to pay for the offerings, to spend a week in prayer with them, and to go on with them to the ritual purifications. He did this gladly. Thus, the most ardent proponents of the Law were reassured (Acts 21:21–26).

The danger from this direction, however grave it may have been, was now removed; but another was about to appear, infinitely more serious. For the feast of Pentecost, numerous pilgrims had come to Jerusalem from all the Jewish communities scattered throughout the Near East, notably from those of Asia Minor. Many of them were well acquainted with the Apostle from having fought him in their cities, driven him from their synagogues, and denounced him to the authorities. Meeting him in the streets of the capital, they were aroused to indignation. Soon a kind of conspiracy developed between them and the Jews of Jerusalem, who regarded the former pupil of the rabban Gamaliel as a traitor and renegade. As the missionary was frequently accompanied by Trophimus, a baptized Greek from Ephesus, they started the rumor circulating that he had brought this pagan into the Temple, which was an obvious crime, and declared as such on the marble plaques at the gates of the Temple court, which forbade the uncircumcised to cross the threshold, under pain of death.

While Paul was in the Temple, completing the proceedings for the offerings and purification of the nazirate, the affair reached its climax, and with unheard-of violence. The Asiatic Jews began running about the Temple courtyard, shouting, "Men of Israel, help. This is the man who teaches all men everywhere against the people and the Law, and this place, and moreover he has brought Gentiles also into the Temple and has desecrated this holy place!" Immediately, there was a indescribable uproar throughout the sanctuary and the colonnades—one of those oriental outbursts, full of sharp cries and vociferous clamor in which, after a short time, no one knows what is going on. The guards had immediately closed the gates. A band of enraged Jews had rushed upon Paul and dragged him into the outer court of the sanctuary. His life was in great danger (Acts 21:27–30).

The intervention of the legionaries saved him. Since Rome had occupied Palestine her officers had learned—sometimes to their cost—that it was necessary to keep a watchful eye on the

Chosen People and their disturbances. Periodically, a riot would break out here and there in Palestine, under pretexts which were not obvious from a Latin point of view. In the year 57 there was already a storm in the air—that storm which some years later, was to burst forth into a tempest and provoke the atrocious Jewish war when, in the year 70, the Romans took and destroyed Jerusalem. Installed in the Antonia, the fortress built by Herod the Great at the northwest corner of the Temple, the tribune kept a relentless watch on what was going on in the courts, holding himself ready to intervene with his soldiers at the first alert. Stairways permitted direct access from the fortress to the Holy Place.

When one of his subordinates came and told Claudius Lysias that there was another commotion in the Temple, that they were shouting and fighting down there, the tribune did not ask himself what might have caused this tumult; he took some centurions and soldiers and plunged into the thick of the melee, at the point from which the most violent outbursts seemed to be coming. Instantaneously, as through a miracle, everything quieted down. At the sight of the breastplates, swords, and red tunics, the most furious rioters became subdued. Paul was delivered, but not for long. Was he the cause of this uproar? Good! Let him be arrested and put in chains now. Later they would see about asking him for explanations, police methods are the same in all ages. Then, turning to the crowd, the tribune tried to obtain some information. Who was this man? What did they have against him? At once the chorus of howls was resumed! Some shouted one thing, some another, to the point of distraction. "Take him to the fortress!" exclaimed the officer. This was no easy matter, for the rioters were pressing on threateningly, with fists raised and with rage on their lips. Amidst the cries for Paul's blood, the soldiers passed Paul along from one to another until he reached the foot of the stairs. Only there was he secure from the mob (Acts 21:31–36).

Peace having been restored Paul was at last able to speak to the tribune. "May I say something to you?" he said. "Does you know Greek?" replied Lysias in astonishment. "Aren't you the Egyptian who recently stirred up sedition and led out into the desert the four thousand assassins?" The good soldier obviously understood nothing of the situation: he had just made his report to Rome on this episode—one of those pretended messianic uprisings such as Judas of Galilee and Theudas had once incited and as Bar Cochebas was later to provoke—and here a new agitator had arisen! It seemed that this one had come, not from Egypt, but from some Hellenistic city in Asia!

Replied Paul: "I am a Jew from Tarsus in Cilicia, a citizen of no insignificant city. But I beg you, let me speak to the people" (Acts 21:37–39).

They brought Paul to the threshold of the Antonia. Standing on the steps, he made a sign with his hand. A great, astonished silence fell, and the Apostle was able to make himself heard. As he expressed himself readily in Aramaic, his audience grew more attentive. For five long minutes there was no interruption. What should he say? Should he present a defense and explain what he was doing in the temple? Should he show that in no way had he profaned the Holy Place? Let others resort to such petty means! He preferred to take this opportunity to give his testimony publicly: to recall the child that he had been, the pupil of Gamaliel, the fanatic of the Law, in order to reveal to all of them the prodigy that had been granted him by Christ Jesus, who had bound him to His cause forever. Deeply impressed, the audience continued to listen. But when, continuing his recital, Paul came to say that the Lord had ordered him to go afar to bring salvation to the pagan nations, the silence ended. There was a wave of threatening cries for Paul's death. To the fanatical Jews his words were intolerable! Salvation for the pagans—sacrilege! Some shook their mantles as if they were about to rend them, as a believer was supposed to do when a blasphemy reached his ears; others picked up dust and threw it in the direction of the impious wretch. Again the tumult began (Acts 22:1–23).

Understanding less and less what was happening, since everyone was speaking in Aramaic, the tribune simply concluded that Paul was the cause of all this trouble...had not his presence alone sufficed to cause the disturbance? It was necessary to find out, once and for all, what he had in his craw; a few good blows with the whip should make him talk. So they brought Paul back to the fortress and the centurion on duty set about his task of having Paul bound with straps for the scourging. But serene in this trial, as he had been in the midst of his worst perils, the little Jew looked the officer in the face and said: "Is it legal for you to scourge a Roman, and that without a trial?" The officer was nonplussed, sensing an embarrassing situation. One of the worst accusations that Cicero had brought against Verres had been exactly this, that he had treated a Roman citizen ignominiously, and the charge had weighed heavily against the Sicilian proprietor. Prudently, the centurion referred the affair to his commander. Claudius Lysias at once returned to speak to Paul. "Tell me, are you a Roman?" "Yes," said Paul. "I obtained this citizenship at a great price. But I am a citizen by birth." Forthwith a man of distinction, Paul was released and treated with consideration. The Empire had its good points (Acts 22:25–29).

From there on the case was outside the competence of a simple company commander; it had to be submitted to the procurator, who was in residence at Caesarea. But it was still essential that this high magistrate be informed on the details and ramifications of the case. Claudius Lysias had a vague idea that it involved some Jewish religious matter; perhaps he would obtain some enlightenment by convening the religious tribunal of the Jews. The Sanhedrin was called together and Paul brought before it.

From the beginning, the hearing threatened to turn out quite badly. Hardly had the Apostle opened his mouth to declare that he had nothing on his conscience, when the high priest, Ananias, had one of his attendants slap him. Outraged, Paul replied with a few sharp words. "God will strike you, you whitewashed wall. Do you sit there to try me by the Law, and in violation of the Law order me to be struck?"

There were shouts of indignation from the audience: "Do you insult God's high priest?" "I did not know, brethren," replied the Apostle, "that he was the high priest; for it is written, 'Thou shalt not speak evil of a ruler of the people.'" Having begun on this note, how was the discussion to end? Paul realized perfectly well the uselessness of any defense. He knew the weak points of his adversaries and skillfully counterattacked.

The Sanhedrin was divided into two groups, the Sadducees and the Pharisees. The former, for the most part, represented the wealthy element of the city, the well-to-do, and, from a spiritual point of view, the easy-going. The Pharisees were, as we know, harsh, rigid, and most severe. Paul was aware that their bone of contention was the doctrine of the future life; the Pharisees believed in the resurrection of the dead and in the judgment of the just and the unjust: the Sadducees did not. "Brethren," he began, "I am a Pharisee, the son of Pharisees; it is about the hope and the resurrection of the dead that I am on trial." It was a shrewd move. Some Sadducees began to protest; Pharisee scribes at once took up the defense of the accused. Soon the session was transformed into a confused and very noisy brawl in which theological arguments crashed around a defendant with whom no one was any longer concerned. Unable to understand any of this, and fearing a chance blow might reach his prisoner, the tribune had him brought back to the Antonia (Acts 23:1-11).

The situation was no clearer than before, but it was a dramatic one for the Apostle. Shut up in the fortress, he was protected by the will of the Roman soldier alone; and all around him was the seething city, bent on murder. Was it the Master's plan for him to be massacred there, in the Temple court, if Lysias should change his mind and deliver him to his adversaries? He had a conviction that his mission was not yet completed, that he still had something to say and do. While he was meditating in this night of anguish, the ineffable image, which he knew so well, appeared to him once more—the Christ. "Be steadfast; for just as thou hast borne witness to me in Jerusalem; bear witness in Rome also" (Acts 23:11).

Events were soon to confirm this prophecy. The disturbance created by the debate in the Sanhedrin was continuing
in the city and excited Jews were accusing various Pharisees of
having permitted the blasphemer to escape sanctions. For
years a ruthless band of fanatics at Jerusalem had been crying
for resistance to the Roman occupation, absolute rigor in matters of faith, and assassination of the lukewarm and treacherous; they were called Zealots, because of their religious zeal, or
else Sicares, because the *sica*, the blade of the Jewish poignard,
was frequently worn under their tunics, and they made use of
it. Was the tribune protecting Paul? And were the authorities
of the Sanhedrin unable to rid the city of this blasphemer?
There was just one solution—a well-aimed blow of the *sica*.
Forty of these extremists bound themselves by oath to carry
out the affair and went to confide their plan to the high priest,
Ananias, who gave his approval. This was the Ananias who
some years later, as if through an answer of Providence, was to
fall under the poignards of the Sicares, who found him too
tepid when the great insurrection broke out.

Never had Paul known such danger. The slightest opportunity, for example, his removal from the Antonia to the palace
of the high priest, would suffice for a knife blade to be planted
between his shoulders in one of the shadowy lanes of the city.
But God was watching over him, and He had other plans. A
nephew of the Apostle, who lived in Jerusalem, had wind of
the plot and acted. Forewarned, the tribune realized that it was
necessary to put an end to this dangerous situation. He gave
orders that this decidedly troublesome defendant should be
transferred immediately to Caesarea (Acts 23:12–22).

Arriving at Caesarea at daybreak, Paul saw in the distance
the gray-green sea shimmering beyond the mauve hills—that
sea on which, he had been assured, he would soon be borne to
Rome for the supreme stage of his mission. Prudent and
human, the tribune Lysias had acted with great correctness; he
had given a horse to the Apostle; and a strong escort of two
hundred foot-soldiers and two hundred and seventy horsemen
protected him from any ambush by the Sicares; as an additional

precaution they had him travel at night. A very equitable report had been sent to the procurator to explain the affair to him and to remit the defendant. But, just the same, it was as a prisoner, uncertain of the fate awaiting him, that Paul was retracing this route which some twelve days before he had followed at liberty. The Gate by which one must strive to enter is always narrow, and the ways of the Lord are arduous (Acts 23:23–33).

Five days later a delegation of the Sanhedrin headed by the high priest appeared at the procurator's tribunal. The procurator was Felix, a former slave whom the influence of his brother Pallas, the famous freedman of the Emperor Claudius, had raised to this high post. Tacitus has given us an unsparing characterization of this individual: "Debauched and cruel, he exercised the royal power with a servile soul. Protected by the enormous fame of his brother, he thought to commit with impunity the worst atrocities." It is just to add, however, that in the present instance this Felix did not appear to be too dreadful. He permitted the defendant to answer freely to the accusations brought against him. Ananias had spared no expense and had hired a Roman lawyer, Tertullus, to present the Jewish case. Paul was able to argue that he had in no way disturbed the peace, that what was involved was merely a religious dispute about the best "way" to reach heaven and that, furthermore, having been denounced by Asiatic Jews, according to the Law he should have been accused by them and not by this delegation of priests. The pleading was skillful and the procurator appeared to be impressed; he sent the case back for supplementary information. In the meanwhile he ordered that the defendant should be treated with courtesy, enjoy comparative freedom, and be able to see his friends (Acts 24:1–23).

This semi-detention was to last for two years. In the eyes of the Lord these two years were certainly not lost, for it was probably during this time that Saint Luke, the beloved physician, who had accompanied his master, consulted many witnesses in preparing to write his Gospel. But Saint Paul was chomping at the bit. Why was Felix holding him? The Book of Acts says, forthrightly, that he was hoping to obtain from him a sizeable *bakshish* in return for his liberty. But Paul refused to understand; it was not to fatten this former slave that God's money was to be spent. From time to time Felix had him brought before him and questioned him on his doctrine. At his side was his wife Drusilla, a young Herodian princess whom he had stolen from her husband Aziz, the Arab king of Emesus; it may be that she felt some sympathy and curiosity about the new faith. But when Paul, refusing to play the game, began speaking of the Christian principles of purity and chastity, the adulterous couple hastily invited him to withdraw (Acts 24:24–26).

Thus the months passed in futile haggling. Then Felix had to leave, having been recalled by Nero in consequence of a minor scuffle at the market in Caesarea; it had ended in a veritable pogrom and the Jews, who were powerful at court, had complained. The new procurator, Porcius Festus, was an upright and conscientious man. On his first trip to Jerusalem Paul's enemies demanded that the prisoner be brought back before the Sanhedrin, which obviously would have made possible his assassination, the plan for which was still cherished by the Sicares. Festus saw through this maneuver and answered that he would look into the affair himself. Once more there were contradictory arguments, rehearings of complaints, and a defense by the Apostle. Realizing that it was a religious affair but not wishing to wrong a Roman citizen, he asked Paul if he would consent to be tried at Jerusalem. The Apostle refused point-blank. Was he afraid that once in the Holy City, the magistrate would yield to pressure and hand him over to the Sanhedrin? Or was he finding that all this had dragged on long enough? "I am standing," he said, "at the tribunal of Caesar; there I ought to be tried." And pronouncing the decisive formula, which for two years he had postponed, he added: "I appeal to Caesar!" Coming from a Roman citizen, the appeal was admissible, and the legal advisers of Festus so declared. "You have appealed to Caesar; to Caesar you shall go," the procurator replied ritually. Thus Paul was to go to Rome. The die had been cast! (Acts 25:1–12).

A few days later, two illustrious visitors arrived: King Agrippa II, great-grandson of Herod the great, and his sister Berenice, the famous beauty whose romance with Titus was to be immortalized by Racine. At Caesarea they were talking about nothing but Paul's appeal to Caesar. Like Drusilla, whose sister she was, Berenice seems to have been curious about religious things. She wanted to see and hear the Apostle. Once more he accepted: was not any occasion valid for announcing his faith and giving testimony? He spoke in the presence of the two princes, Festus, and a whole assembly of officers and notables who had come to greet the Herodians. And he spoke with a fullness and eloquence which were even more striking than usual. His voice became fiery. His words touched their hearts. It was his whole life that he was evoking, his complete conviction that he was declaring; and he was doing so for the last time, as he well knew, on this holy ground. In vain the procurator sought to calm him. "Paul, you are mad; your great learning is driven you to madness." But Paul went on. "I am not mad . . . the king knows about these things . . . Do you believe the prophets, King Agrippa? I know that you do." Embarrassed and confused and feeling his Jewish blood rushing to his face, the Herodian prince extricated himself with a subterfuge: "In a short while you would persuade me to be a Christian!" Berenice was listening, silent and thoughtful. In the hubbub that followed the conclusion of the session, she leaned toward her brother and said: "This man has done nothing to deserve death or imprisonment." And summing up the general opinion, Agrippa said to Festus: "This man might have been set at liberty if he had not appealed to Caesar."

But by making an appeal to an imperial tribunal, Paul had opened—and he well knew it—a new chapter in his destiny.

The Prisoner of Christ

In the spring of the year 60, the *Castor and Pollux*, a mixed cargo ship in service on the Egyptian line, arrived in the Bay of Naples; bad weather had forced the ship to linger at Malta, but the favorable south wind having risen, it had finally reached its destination, sailing via Syracuse and Reggio Calabria (Acts 28:11–13). There before Paul, what is perhaps the most beautiful bay in Europe, opened wide the arms of its yellow hills where parasol pines raised their black peaks. Vesuvius was smoking, but the light mist shrouded its threat with a dream-like halo. Everything that wealth and taste could accomplish seemed to be concentrated there, in this little corner of land bathed by the sparkling sea, where famous cities displayed their marble villas amidst gardens of cypress and roses: Baiae, Herculaneum, Naples, Pompeii. But a few feet away in the poorer neighborhoods of the ports, misery, human agony, injustice, and hate were rampant in the louse and cockroach-ridden hovels. And everywhere, among both the rich and the poor, there was anguish, an anguish ill-concealed by frenzied rejoicing; an anguish of living and an anguish of dying, which could not be relieved by the hundred oriental cults whose temples and ceremonial halls arose at every crossing; nor by the pure water of Isis, nor by the blood of the bull Mithra. What better entrance could the Apostle have chosen into this world of Rome toward which his thoughts had been turning for years, a world of glory and secret misery, which had been waiting unwittingly for some-one to come and tell it of the way, the life, and the truth?

The voyage from Palestine to Italy had taken a long time and had been full of exciting incidents. Since autumn had arrived and the ships following direct routes had suspended service, it had been necessary to take a vessel which followed the coast of Asia Minor. Under the benevolent surveillance of a centurion named Julius, Paul had embarked together with some people of less importance. They had permitted him to take along three of his disciples as secretaries: Luke, the faithful Timothy, and Aristarchus, a Christian from Thessalonica. They had cast off the moorings and the wind had filled the sails as if an omen of an adventurous voyage.

And adventurous it was—a zigzag wandering voyage— which Saint Luke reported with such lively detail in the Book of Acts that Admiral Nelson one day declared he had learned much of his profession from reading these few pages. They had first anchored at Sidon, the Phoenician port, where the benevolent Julius had permitted his prisoner to go and pay a visit to the Christian community there. Then, setting sail once more, the captain attempted to head directly for Asia Minor. But contrary winds had forced him to run in behind its great cliffs, and to touch at Myra. There in the great Lycian port they had had the good luck to find an Alexandrian ship about to leave for Italy. The centurion had his entire bank of soldiers and prisoners transferred to it. They had started off again, but the winds continued unfavorable. Progressing slowly, gropingly, rolling and pitching heavily, the ship had difficulty in coming as far as Cnidus, and it had been unable to approach the harbor. It had therefore been necessary to let the ship run before the wind to Crete, where they had finally been able to anchor in a mediocre harbor called Fair Havens, an apparently misleading name.

During these long days in which they were crowded together on the narrow bridge of the ship, Paul and his companions seem to have become acquainted with the sailors, the military escort, and the passengers. And as always, the personality of the great Apostle had made an impression. This had been evident in an incident which took place on the coast of Crete, an incident which could have turned into a tragic accident. Finding the harbor at Fair Havens unsatisfactory, the captain had decided to make for Phoenix, which was more sheltered. Paul, who had acquired a knowledge of the perils of the sea during his many voyages, had pointed out that the move might be ticklish; they had not listened to him. They had passed the little isle of Cauda on their portside at full speed, without being able to even attempt to make a stop there. They had had to resort to emergency measures, to gird the ship with cables, put out the sea anchor, and then to throw overboard the cargo and even some of the rigging. For four-teen days and fourteen nights this nightmare had continued, without stars or sun; hardly anyone had eaten during this time! Their nerves were frazzled. Paul alone had retained his bal-ance. Commanding the attention of all, even of the frightened captain, he had announced in the name of God, that catastro-phe would be avoided, that the lives of all of them would be saved and that only the ship would perish. And thus it had happened; shortly afterward, the ship had run aground, and had been broken up by the storm, but none of the 276 passen-gers was reported missing.

Thus God had shown once more that His witness was in His hands, and that the Holy Spirit alone was directing his course. On two other occasions He was to publicly manifest His power through the Apostle. At Malta, where they had been cast by the shipwreck, they were all drying themselves around a great fire, when Paul, having picked up an armful of dry wood, had been bitten by a viper, which sank its fangs in his hand; but while all those present were looking with horror at this man who was so obviously cursed that divine justice was going to destroy him by poison just after he had escaped from shipwreck, the Apostle, with a calm gesture, had shaken the beast into the fire and had suffered no harm.

And another time at Malta, where they had spent all the latter part of the winter, the divine power within him had been manifested in the cure of an old man belonging to the cream of Maltese society. The father of that first magistrate of the island who had so warmly received the castaways having fallen very ill, Paul, who in the course of his life had always shown himself rather economical with regard to miracles, had gone and cured him with a word. And he cured not only this man, but many of the other sick people on the island, as if it had seemed necessary to him to make everyone understand that wherever he went the Lord would be with him, and that if he had to carry out his sacrifice it would be according to the will of God (Acts 27:1–28:10).

Now Paul was following the Appian Way, amidst that stream of Phoenician merchants, Italian peasants, Greek or Thracian slaves, dark skins and light skins, which flowed up and down on this road, perhaps the most frequented of the Empire. Armored guards kept a check on the traffic and were especially vigilant with regard to the heavy carts bringing in wheat to Rome. From Pozzzuoli, where Paul and his companions had disembarked, to the Eternal City was a journey of four or five days on foot; at the stopping places, numerous inns afforded the travelers a rather noisy lodging; and thus Christ's conqueror—small, sickly, covered with dust, and still chained to two soldiers—arrived in this capital of the ancient world where his words and his sacrifice were to complete the triumph of the Revolution of the Cross.

But from the instant when he first set foot on Italian soil, the Apostle received great encouragement: even at Pozzuoli some Christians came to greet him; the Church was present there, alive and growing, as he had found at Sidon or in Crete, and as he dreamed of seeing it everywhere. The evening of their third stage, at the place called the "Forum of Appias," in the heart of the Pontine marches, there was a whole delegation of Christians from Rome to greet and entertain him—with the permission of Julius, the benevolent centurion. These faithful souls had traveled more than thirty-five miles on foot to greet him whose high deeds were not unknown to any member of the church; and ten miles farther on, at Three Taverns, there was a little crowd which waited and listened to him avidly. For all this Paul gave thanks to the Lord; he felt completely comforted (Acts 28:11–15).

He had already known it for a long time: the Church at Rome was strong and flourishing—that splendid community to which he had sent from Corinth the fullest and most profound of all his letters; and here was the proof of that development. What is certain is that this first Christian community was implanted in the extremely numerous Jewish colony, which was distributed in the Transtevere, the Subura, the

Campus Martius quarter, and the vicinity of the Porta Capena. We have the proof of this in a line from the historian Suetonius who relates that under the reign of the Emperor Claudius— probably about the year 48—there were disturbances in Rome's Jewish colony "at the instigation of Chrestos"—a vague expression, and written by an uninformed person, but which gives us some idea of the reality of the incident. And this fact is confirmed by the Book of Acts, in which Aquila and Priscilla, Paul's friends at Corinth and later at Ephesus, appear as Jews driven from the capital by Claudius.

Into this primitive Church, still more or less shut up in the narrow framework of the Jewish colony, there had arrived, at a date which we cannot precisely determine, a man whose glorious figure was to shine forth over Rome from century to century; this was Peter, the rock upon which it had been said the entire Church would be founded. The sojourn of the Prince of the Apostles at Rome, which has been a great subject of debate between Catholics and Protestants since the Reformation, is no longer doubted today; and the German Protestant historian, Lietzmann, in his great work, *Petrus and Paulus in Rom*, after having reviewed all the texts from the first to the third century which affirm or presume this residence, and all the archeological documents, concluded in its favor. We know, besides, that the most recent excavations under the Basilica of Saint Peter are constantly bringing forward new arguments in favor of the thesis which the tradition of the Catholic Church has always maintained; and on several occasions, in reporting the results of the work then in progress, His Holiness Pius XII had solemnly declared that Saint Peter's presence and death in Rome cannot be denied. Quitting Jerusalem permanently after the council of the year 49–50, the Prince of the Apostles was installed for a time at Antioch, and then had sojourned at Corinth; Saint Paul's first epistle to the Christians of that city seems to allude to his presence there. Then he had arrived in the capital. Rather old at this date—about seventy undoubtedly—loaded with honors, an old soldier of the Gospel in whose face the faithful still saw the reflection of the Transfiguration, Peter was to exercise over this young Roman Church the prestige of a soul inhabited by the Most High.

But it is certain that the evangelical sowing had not been restricted to Jewish circles. In the enormous cosmopolitan city which Rome then was, inhabited by more than a million souls, where peoples of all races were thrown together, where so many men and women were distraught by a religious anxiety and were seeking in many numerous doctrines, rites, and superstitions for the answer to the great problems, it would have been quite surprising if groups of Christians had not developed. Jewish monotheism itself had already won some proselytes among the pagans, even in the court of the Emperor, where Poppaea, the titular mistress of Nero (who had just stolen her from her husband), was practicing, if not the morality of Yahweh, at least some Jewish observances.

It should be noted that at this moment—at the beginning of the year 60—there was not even a thought of a persecution by the Roman Empire against the Christians. In the eyes of the police they constituted a small Asian sect among many others; provided that they remained quiet, there was no intention of disturbing them. Moreover, the reign of Nero had not yet reached the tragic turning after which the bloody frenzy was to begin; the royal maniac's crimes were still confined to a limited circle: Britannicus, his young rival, Agrippina, his troublesome mother, and a few consular officials and freedmen; public opinion had not attached much importance to these executions. Thus, in the general tranquility, the Church must have prospered and her preaching must have reached quarters which were entirely different from those of the ghettoes.

Was it not of these Gentiles who had been his life-long concern that Paul was thinking as he passed the Porta Capena? If, by demanding to be brought to the tribunal of Caesar, he had intended to be taken to the capital, it was because he knew that an immense task required his presence there. To complete the triumph of the Cross, it was necessary that it be raised in that crossroads of the nations which was the Eternal City. Peter, a rock of faith, had founded the Church there on unshakable foundations; now it was necessary for it to expand and conquer; it was to this task that Paul, at the side of his elder, was now to apply himself.

That this was his true mission, events—a manifestation of the divine will—were to prove to him once more, if indeed he needed such proof. On arriving in Rome, Paul was delivered by the good centurion, Julius, to the officer of praetorian guard in charge of prisoners referred to the Emperor's tribunal. His Roman citizenship, probably cited in a favorable report sent by the procurator Festus, won him some degree of respect; he was placed under military surveillance, *custodia Militaris*; that is, he would be authorized to live in town in a friendly house not far from the praetorian barracks, to receive visits, to correspond with anyone he wished; but he was to have near him at all times a guard who held him by a small chain fixed to his wrist, and he did not have the right to leave the city. This semi-captivity lasted for two years: Caesar's justice was by no means hasty.

Just three days after his arrival, Paul had wished to resume his apostolate. He had sent messages to the Jewry of Rome, summoning the leaders of his compatriots to confer with him; they came and, through an entire day, they listened and argued. But this was without result. On hearing the Apostle speak of Jesus and explain how His words opened the Kingdom of Heaven to those who followed Him, some were convinced, but the majority remained skeptical. The discussion ended in confusion. By attempting to convert the Jews, the Apostle of the Gentiles had apparently blundered. He realized this and murmured what the prophet Isaiah had said of these people: "With their ears they have been hard of hearing, and their eyes they have closed!" And once again he concluded: "This salvation of God has been sent to the Gentiles, and they will listen to it" (Acts 28:16–29).

Then, leaving the first Christian nucleus, directed by Peter, to work especially among the Jews, Paul devoted himself to sowing the good seed in all the other ground which he could reach. We do not know of any period in this full and noble existence which gives such an impression of plenitude, accomplishment, and grandeur as these two years of captivity. It is in bondage that the nobler man feels free, because then his liberty comes only from the Spirit, and the servitudes which are imposed on him are accepted as occasions for surpassing achievement and total realization. Lest the good people who had offered him a room be troubled by the constant coming and going of his guards and visitors, Paul rented a house where he could live with his friends. And this semi-prison became a center of propaganda, a consecrated place from which the Word of God spread through Rome.

Around him was grouped an entire company of followers; there was Luke, naturally, who in the course of these two years wrote his Gospel and the book of the Acts of the Apostles; there was the beloved Timothy, "true son according to the faith"; Mark, who, having returned, had won pardon for his desertion from the first mission and who, friendly with both Peter and Paul, was ready to serve as a bond between the two pillars of the Church; and Aristarchus, Tychicus, and many others. The authority of this prisoner, who was constantly fettered to a guard, impressed everyone. The praetorians who guarded him and to whom he spoke of Christ, were moved and some of them were converted—which led the Apostle to say that his captivity was turning out to the advantage of the Gospel. People from all walks of life, both men and women, came to see him, tormented by religious anxiety; and many of them went back to their home at peace, won over to Christ. Among these were some aristocrats: Eubulus, Pudens, and Linus; this latter was none other than Saint Linus, a pope, the first successor of Saint Peter. Even in the "house of Caesar" the number of Christians was increasing. Invincible power of the Spirit: this man in chains was radiant with God's freedom.

His activities extended even further. In his little house near the praetorian barracks, the Apostle's thoughts passed beyond

Rome to the immense empire in which he had sowed the seed of the Gospel. He was less free than ever from that care which had always haunted him, his concern for the churches that he had founded. To several of them he wrote letters, those simple and beautiful "Epistles of the captivity," infused with more warmth than the great dogmatic Epistles, as if the maturity of his fifty years and the difficult situation in which he found himself had made Christ's conqueror more tender, more human. And from these distant churches messages arrived bringing testimony of touching fidelity. This prison room became a center of the world.

One day Paul saw a wretched slave, Onesimus, enter his home; he had fled from his master, after having robbed him, and was stranded in Rome, among the dregs of the population. The Apostle received him with that wonderful charity which he always practiced toward the weak and the vanquished. He spoke to him so effectively that he won him for Christ and baptized him. Now, the master of Onesimus, Philemon, was a Christian; here was an excellent occasion for demonstrating to all that in the faith of the Gospels there was "neither slave nor freedman." And Paul sent the slave to his master with a note which is a marvel of tact, delicacy, and fraternal love, asking not only that he be pardoned, but that he should be treated as a brother. And thus it happened.

Another time it was a more important personage who arrived at the Apostle's door: Epaphras, a disciple whom Paul had left in the distant city of Colossae, on the borders of Armenia, to guide the Christian community. He had come to impart his anxieties; the faith of the Christians there seemed to be deviating in the direction of strange beliefs, a suspect asceticism, speculations, and superstitions—a sort of illuminism more or less foreshadowing what was later known as Gnosticism. Paul immediately called a secretary and dictated a letter to the Colossians to put them on guard against the snares of the devil, who is always ready to make use of good intentions in order to destroy man's body and to warp his mind.

And once again—and this was still more touching—Paul saw appear on his threshold, a Christian wearing the Macedonian costume which he knew so well. The poor little church of Philippi, founded by him at the time of his second mission, had learned that he was a prisoner and unfortunate and that, because he was unable to work, he was suffering poverty; they had made a collection and had sent Epaphroditus to bring the modest proceeds to Rome. Moved by this gesture he at once wrote to his beloved Philippians a letter of thanks whose sincere and noble accents still touches our hearts.

The two years of this amazing period came to an end. In his note to Philemon, the Apostle had let it be understood that he was in high hopes of being freed shortly. The Praetorian Prefect was the upright Burrus, whom Nero had not yet replaced with the infamous Tigellinus. Roman justice was strict but equitable. As Paul's dossier contained nothing opposed to public order or the security of the state, and as no Jewish accuser had presented himself, the imperial magistrates had him released, probably in the course of the winter of the year 62–63.

"Bear Witness in Rome" (Acts 23:11)

It was the following year that the drama began to develop, the first act of the great drama of the persecution: it began fortuitously, although opposition between Rome and the Cross was evidently inscribed in the designs of Providence. During the night of the 18th or 19th of July of the year 64, a violent fire broke out in the city and soon assumed threatening proportions. Fed by the stores of oil in the business district, where it had originated, and spread by a strong wind, it had reached, one after another, eleven of the fourteen quarters which made up Rome. For 150 hours, terror reigned; shouting mobs ran through the streets like panicked insects, vainly seeking the way to safety. Precious souvenirs of the past, such as the temple of Vesta, caved in amid the acrid smoke. No count was made of the dead. And for a long time after the Vigiles' firemen had brought the disaster under control, a nauseating odor lingered over the whole city, a catastrophe suggesting the end of the world.

Was the disaster accidental? Fire found an easy prey in the wooden tenement districts which made up the city! However, the Roman people did not accept this explanation. They were soon saying that the fire had been reported to break out at eight places simultaneously, that men had been seen carrying torches, spreading the fire instead of combating it; and a culprit's name was on everyone's lips. There was a storm brewing in Rome; in the two years that had passed since that winter of 62–63, when Paul had left, events had moved rapidly. The reign of Nero had already entered into that bloody orgy and maniacal fury which history has recorded. With Burrus dead, Seneca in disgrace, and the star of the abject Tigellinus on the rise, crimes were becoming commonplace. One had horrified the mind of the people; Nero had repudiated his legitimate wife, Octavia, the daughter of Claudius, and after covering her name with the foulest calumny, had had her executed; the spectacle of this severed head presented to the favorite had been terrifying.

Rumors spread: Nero was said to have remarked several times: "They have not yet learned that nothing is impossible for the Prince!" And on the eve of the fire he was said to have cited this line from Euripides: "Let the whole earth fall prey to fire!" It was also said—and indeed there was no limit to these rumors—that during the disaster he sat perched at the top of the Maecenatian Tower, and dressed in theatrical costume and with a lyre in his hand, chanted a poem he had composed on the fire at Troy. It was soon generally admitted that he was the person responsible for the disaster.

Nero was frightened now, terrified at the wrath of the people. He needed a culprit, a diversion—and at once. The Christians could serve him here. Why not? The crowds knew of their existence, though what was known of them was merely rumor; there is nothing new in the terrible tendency of the masses to peddle the basest libel about something of which they are ignorant. The Christians exchanged a kiss of peace at the beginning of their meetings. From this it was presumed that they engaged in infamous relations. They asserted that the bread and wine with which they made their communion were the body and blood of their God. This led to an accusation of ritual crimes and cannibalism; it was said that they covered a young child with flour, slit its throat, and passionately devoured it. Pointing them out to the angry crowd, one was certain to find willing ears; besides, as they were relatively few in number and without defense, the operation could be carried out without difficulty.

Accused of professing "hatred of the human race," they were arrested in a vast police round-up, tortured in order to force the weaker to betray their brethren, and, without trial, were sent out to execution. On August 15 in the year 64, less than a month after the fire, the festival of horror began. The most horrible inventions that could be imagined by a sadist who possessed complete power were realized in a nightmare fantasy. It was not enough to torture, decapitate, and crucify the victims in the imperial circus, which was on the site of the present Basilica of Saint Peter. Hunts were conducted in the imperial parks, with the prey consisting of Christians sewed up in the skins of beasts, to be torn to pieces by the Molossian hunting dogs. The most obscene fables of mythology were staged with Christians as the actors—submitted to every kind of outrage. And at night, in Nero's gardens, along the paths where the crowned fool, clad in a coachman's cloak, laughed as he drove his chariot, to light his way they set fire to tall torches of pitch and resin—which were human beings.

The persecution was not confined to these abominable sports for the amusement of the city's herds. It broke out in all the provinces where Christianity existed: the First Epistle of Saint Peter, addressed to the faithful of Pontus, Galatia, Cappadocia, and Bithynia, makes reference to these trials. All of Asia Minor was affected by police measures; it was at this time that Saint Paul fell into the hands of the executioners.

What had he been doing since he left Rome? We are no longer informed in detail on his apostolate, for the Book of Acts stops at the beginning of his first detention and the information that can be drawn from the last epistle is far from replacing Saint Luke's lively reports on the earlier periods. Perhaps he had gone to evangelize Spain; he had been planning this for a long time, and had even imparted his plan to the faithful at Rome (Rom. 15:24–28). Many of the Church Fathers, such as Saint Cyril, Saint Jerome, and Saint John Chrysostom, speak of this Spanish voyage as a certainty.

Then the great, tireless traveler had traversed the entire breadth of the *Imperium romanum* and returned to Asia Minor, as he had promised his beloved Philemon. He had undoubtedly stopped at Ephesus, to see once more that Christian community which had cost him so much pain and effort; on departing after this visit of inspection, he had left behind there his dear disciple Timothy, and, as his son according to the Spirit was still young and had remained somewhat timid, and as there was some risk that he might be discouraged by the difficulties of his task, Paul had written him, from his next stop ping place, a letter full of encouragement and advice, explaining how he must combat certain erratic tendencies in the Ephesians and must maintain strong discipline and an eminent sense of responsibility within the community, especially among the priests and deacons.

Where had he gone then? Probably to Macedonia; to Greece, too, and perhaps to Crete, the long island at which he had merely touched during his great voyage to Rome, but where, it seems, a vigorous Church had developed, at the head of which he left his friend Titus; to him, too, he sent a beautiful letter, full of useful advice. It has been asked whether he may not have sojourned again in Illyria, pushing on as far as Dalmatia and thus realizing an old dream which he had cherished in the Epistle to the Romans: to trace a road for Christ direct from Jerusalem to Rome, through Greece and the Adriatic. Thus, while a terrible tempest was shaking the whole Church, at a time when merely to proclaim oneself a Christian meant danger of death, the intrepid missionary, with his confidence in the final victory intact, continued to cultivate the Roman soil and to sow the seed of the Gospel, leaving its growth to Christ.

But the hour was approaching when another testimony than those of word and deed would be asked of him. It was in the course of the year 66, probably toward the end of summer, that the hour struck. Paul had returned to Asia Minor, to that city of Troas from which he had once set out to conquer Europe. At Troy he had stopped at the house of a friend named Carpus, where he had installed himself with his personal effects, his clothes and papers. But at Ephesus, during his last stay, he had unmasked and anathematized two Christian traitors, the apostates Alexander and Hymeneus (1 Tim. 1:19–20). One of them, Alexander, a metal-worker, denounced him (2 Tim. 4:14–15). Arrested suddenly—he had not even time to take his old Cilician cloak, which he kept with him constantly, nor his books and papers—he was at first transferred to Ephesus, the capital of the Asiatic province and the residence of the governor. He could count on some friends there. The weaker souls were terrified by the persecution; some, especially those in official positions, who until then had been closely associated with the Apostle, ostensibly turned away from him (2 Tim. 1:15): these renegades depressed him. On the other hand, there were instances of remarkable courage; Aquila and Priscilla remained faithful to themselves, that is to say, perfect; the beloved Timothy, in spite of his distress, proved himself worthy of the confidence which his master had always shown in him; and Onesiphorus especially, a disciple who is somewhat obscure until this time, manifested a firm heroism and limitless devotion which were praised by Paul (2 Tim. 1:16–18).

Embarking at Ephesus, the Apostle was sent to Rome; he well knew why.

Saint Paul's second captivity in no way resembled the first. In two years everything had changed. The political atmosphere had become oppressive, insufferable; a plot against Nero had just fallen through, and the protagonists, among them the philosopher Seneca and the poet Lucan, had been ordered to open their veins. Thereafter, by virtue of the "law of majesty," trials and executions had proceeded at an ever-increasing pace; Petronius, his master's companion in debauchery, had just become his victim; Poppaea herself the favorite, had died as a result of her master's brutalities—killed by him, it was said, with a kick in the small of the back. The people were growing weary. They bore Nero no good will for the sums spent in luxuriously rebuilding the city, nor for the free distribution of flour and oil, nor for the incessantly repeated games, and it was no longer amusing to see Christians crucified at the crossroads, agonizing for hours, or to see young Christians burned alive. In these last eighteen months of Nero's reign—he was to be assassinated in the year 68—hatred and terror were rampant in Rome.

For Paul there could no longer be any question of the gentler treatment he had known previously; it was not military custody now, but the dungeon. His confinement was so restricted that his friends had the greatest difficulty in reaching him. The first who succeeded was Onesiphorus, who had been so heroic and generous at Ephesus; some Roman Christians who had been converted by the Apostle also succeeded in getting in touch with him; among these were Eubulus, Pudentius, the future Pope Linus, and a courageous woman, Claudia. But others whom the great missionary had cherished gave way and took flight—Demas, for example—and Paul was grieved by this; Saint Luke, the beloved physician, remained at his post, faithful to the end.

His surroundings were deplorable. The dungeon was a hideous place; Roman tradition would have it that the Apostle was confined in the subbasement of the Mamertine prison, together, we are told, with Saint Peter, and it is impossible to escape a feeling of anguish as one descends the steep stairs that lead to this miserable hole. What must it have been in those days, when filthy vermin swarmed in the dark, when the captives suffered a daily torture from hunger and cold! Paul had not even his old cloak to protect himself; this had remained at Troy, with Carpus, and his touching words in reclaiming it, in his letter to Timothy, clearly indicate how much this man of iron must have been suffering.

It is not surprising that, in such conditions, his intrepid soul yielded a little, and that in the second letter to Timothy, which was written at this time, he did not conceal the fact that his thoughts were not happy. But it was not for himself that he was afraid. What clutched at his heart was not the approach of his own hour. Of what was he thinking? Of nothing but his work, of the Church, of those communities born of his hands, which had been the supreme concern of his whole life. Almost totally abandoned and awaiting martyrdom, he sent to his beloved son a spiritual testament in which he explained to him that it was necessary to maintain the doctrine of Christ firmly against all deviations, to direct unfailingly the communities entrusted to him, to give himself entirely to the apostolic ministry: the hero was looking beyond his approaching death to the future of his cause, a future full of light. As for himself, without any illusions as to the fate which awaited him, he exclaimed in a sublime act of faith: "As for me, I am already being poured out in sacrifice, and the time of my deliverance is at hand. I have fought the good fight, I have finished the course, I have kept the faith. For the rest, there is laid up for me a crown of justice, which the Lord, the just Judge, will give to me in that day; yet not to me only, but also to those who love His coming" (2 Tim. 4: 6–8).

It is with these words, beautiful in their simplicity, that the Apostle's message ends. Of his end we know nothing certain. Before what tribunal was he brought? Of what was he accused? Who pronounced the death sentence? We do not know. The very date of his martyrdom is a matter of debate, and according to the first historians of the Church, varies from the end of the year 66 to the beginning of 68; the best informed, Eusebius, accepts the year 67. It has often been maintained that the date coincided with that on which the other great pillar of the Church, Saint Peter, was broken. But while the Galilean fisherman, a humble beggar, knew the torture of the Cross, which, out of humility, he asked to suffer with his head down, in order that he should not appear to be equaling his divine Master, Paul, as a Roman citizen, had the privilege of being decapitated.

A very ancient tradition, which has practically never been questioned, identifies the spot where the Apostle of the Nations baptized the pagan soil of Rome with his blood. It is an hour's walk from the walls of the city, in a secluded valley surrounded with wooded hills. There are some springs there, which won it the name of *Aquae Salviae,* "healthful waters"; in our day it is known as Three Fountains. There are three churches there and a community of Trappists maintains a silent vigil of prayers and fidelity.

On the old road to Ostia, which still winds along not far off the modern highway, we may imagine the cortège that led the great witness to the supreme libation one cool autumn morning. A platoon of praetorians under the command of a centurion came to fetch him from his dungeon. The little Jew was pale, sickly, gaunt from hunger and confinement; his head was bare and his beard was growing white, but his glance was still unvanquished, the glance, not of a captive, but of a conqueror. The wind from the sea drove the clouds in a course like that of the wrathful horsemen whom Saint John the Apostle was later to picture in his Apocalypse. The buskins of the guards beat out a cadence on the paving stones, and one could hear the branches of the great pines creaking. A whole troop silently accompanied the condemned man; there were his friends Luke, Linus, Pudentius, Eubulus, and perhaps Mark and Timothy, who had responded to their leader's final call; there were some idlers, too, some of those contemptible curiosity-seekers whom an execution always attracts, as blood draws flies; there were, too, no doubt, the old Jewish adversaries of the Apostle, who had come out from Subura and Transtevere to witness what they believed was his final defeat.

On reaching the place appointed for the execution, the centurion had the condemned man bound to a post, to receive once more the customary scourging; then an under-officer raised his sword and the saint's head rolled, in a double jet of blood.

Countless traditions, more pious than authentic, have sought to add marvelous details to this scene, which must have been so simple. It is told that, on falling, the martyr's head bounced three times and that three fountains had immediately sprung from the earth—the three fountains which one still sees there; or else that the lips of the decapitated murmured the name of Jesus in Aramaic. We are assured, too, that the band with which they covered his eyes was borne away by the angels and returned to the pious woman who had lent it to him; and again, that, at the instant the fatal blow fell, a dazzling light appeared in the sky, a light as brilliant and supernatural as that which had struck down the enemy of Christ on the road to Damascus, thirty years before. Pious legends! The stark reality is worth far more than these embellishments.

On the road to Ostia, about five hundred yards from the gate of the city, was a private cemetery belonging to a Christian family; Paul's friends and disciples transported his mortal remains there. A monument was erected there which was judiciously given the form of a victory trophy; the priest Gaius, at the beginning of the third century, gave a description of it. A simple epitaph was engraved on it: *Paul, Apostle, martyr.* This sufficed; therein all was said.

Paul, Apostle, martyr... Yes, this tells the tale. In these three words is assumed and summed up the prodigious destiny of the little Jew of Tarsus, whom the personal will of God made the most extraordinary of all His witnesses. Since that splendid hour at the height of noon, when, on the sandy trail, Jesus appeared before the prostrate Saul, until this gray morning when, on the road to Ostia, his blood was poured out as a libation, not a day had passed which he had not given to the cause of Christ; not a single thought or effort which had not tended to establish His glory. Martyrdom was the normal conclusion of this destiny, for it would have been inadmissible that he should not consummate his total sacrifice—he who had wished to complete in his flesh what was lacking in the sufferings of Christ and to be nailed to the Cross with Him. But there was to be an immense number of martyrs in the Church's history; their blood was to be, according to the famous expression of Tertullian, "the seed of Christians"; among them Paul occupies a unique, exceptional place, which the Church has always acknowledged.

An apostle, yes. He was an apostle, as he said himself, and as all Christian tradition has proclaimed. As much as those dozen Galilean fishermen and farmers whom Jesus had appointed to follow Him, the Rabbi Saul had a right to this title and he laid claim to it legitimately. It is indeed false to pretend, as some do, that he was the inventor of Christianity and that the teaching of Jesus would not exist without him; for the Gospel which he preached was substantially the same as that of the other Apostles and he did no more than define, clarify, and distribute the treasures which the Master Himself had given. But it is beyond doubt that, without him, Christianity would not be exactly as we know it. It has been said of him that he was "the first after the Unique"; his role was such that we cannot understand Jesus and His Word without referring to the saintly genius of Tarsus—to his message and to his deeds.

It is in his letters that we must find and hear Paul's message—in those imperishable letters which we have merely touched on in these pages, giving their essential contents and the circumstance in which they were written. It is to these we must resort, and the revelations enclosed there will emerge with their great shattering bursts of light. Is it not true that at Mass, when the reading of the Epistle brings us some brief passage, our impression is one of an immediate shock, which reaches the depth of our souls and suddenly illuminates the anguished darkness of the world and of ourselves?

The centuries flow by and events move on, but the message of Saint Paul remains; nothing shall ever invalidate it. For anyone who considers his example, for anyone who hears his words, there emerge lessons which are ever new.

To the helpless feeling of negation and absurdity, which is, for all of us, the worst temptation of the conscience, Paul opposes the unshakable certainty that there is a supernatural explanation, an ultimate revelation, which definitively sets forth the meaning of life.

In the face of the great treason of man, that universal oblivion into which the world is plunging, he declares, with unique persuasive power, the reality of a presence which no philosophy can abolish and whose infinite mercy no treason can discourage.

Before that feeling of despair which man draws from the very heart of his condition, and which penetrates the inmost fibers of an era like ours, what he says, repeats, and proclaims is that there is no ineluctable fatality, that redeemed man has a promise of glory: "O death, where is thy victory? O death, where is thy sting?"

And in a universe of hatred and violence, the positive contribution of the great Apostle is something he has received from Christ Himself and has expressed in deathless words; the message of Charity, the omnipotence of Love.

For us Christians, Saint Paul is unquestionably the most wonderful example of that pure and ardent flame which Christ Jesus can light in the souls of those who love Him. And even for those who do not share his faith, he remains a genius, a hero, the champion of causes which are more precious than life itself, a man who is a credit to mankind.